A Fool's Guide to Landlording

By

Tony Midea and Sandra Midea

authorHOUSE

1663 LIBERTY DRIVE, SUITE 200
BLOOMINGTON, INDIANA 47403
(800) 839-8640
www.authorhouse.com

This book is a work of non-fiction. Names of people and places have been changed to protect their privacy.

© 2004 Tony Midea and Sandra Midea.
All Rights Reserved.

No part of this book may be reproduced, stored in a retrieval system, or transmitted by any means without the written permission of the author.

First published by AuthorHouse 06/23/04

ISBN: 1-4184-1727-0 (e)
ISBN: 1-4184-1728-9 (sc)

Library of Congress Control Number: 2004093253

Printed in the United States of America
Bloomington, Indiana

This book is printed on acid-free paper.

Table of Contents

Chapter 1
What Are You Thinking? 1

Chapter 2
How to Buy Your First House? 5

Chapter 3
The "Fix-Up" 15

Chapter 4
Finding the "Ideal" Tenant 31

Chapter 5
The Ground Rules 49

Chapter 6
Eviction 59

Chapter 7
Taxes and Insurance 71

Chapter 8
Internet Sites and Books for Landlords 85

Chapter 9
Horror Stories 97

Chapter 10
Conclusions 145

Chapter 11
Sources of Additional Information 147

Chapter 1

What Are You Thinking?

Don't!!! Just do not do it!!!! Stop right now, toss this book away and slap yourself silly until you get all thoughts of being a landlord out of your head. Believe me, this self-imposed punishment will pale in comparison to the ugly world you seem hell bent on entering.

Oh, I know, you think that you'll make some money off of your investment, that investing in real estate is safer than the stock market, that you'll lower your taxes, and an endless line of other justifications that make becoming a landlord seem like a sensible thing to do. Maybe, maybe not. If you're lucky, financially you'll break even. Chances are you'll lose money, and more importantly, your faith in human kind. And hey, you probably don't have enough stress in your life, so why not ratchet the stress level up a few notches? You didn't want to live forever anyway, did you? Plus, a full head of hair is overrated. It'll just go gray anyway.

So what makes us such experts to be writing a book and dissing your ambitions? After all, what about those TV real estate gurus that say anyone can do it? Well, we did more than dip our toe into the rental game. We dove in full force and came out of it bloodied and battered. We still have one single family home that we rent, but when our reliable tenant moves on, we will have none.

Stop reading NOW. Go to the chapter on horror stories (Chapter 9). There are several movies waiting to be made. If you still have the stamina, and desire to start this endeavor after reading that chapter, come on back. I'll understand if you don't return. Thanks for buying our book and have a nice life.

Damn, you're back. Just don't say we didn't warn you, my friend.

First, a little about our aspirations to help you understand how and why we did the rental thing. We had hoped to buy several properties, hopefully gain the experience needed to move on to multi-unit complexes and eventually leave conventional employment behind us. My wife and I both have some skill in home repair and maintenance, have an understanding of business and taxes, and generally work well with other people.

So, if you bought this book because you wanted to get advice from some professional real estate guru, well, you screwed up. Take heart, though, I've read all of those books by these "qualified" characters. While they give SOME good advice, I thought they tried too hard to sell their ideas. The business is not as easy as they claim, has substantial downside risk, and is not as profitable as they claim. At least not for common "Joes" like us. This book gives you the "man on the street" experience.

Anyway, back to the background story. At the time we did not have kids, and we paid horrendous tax bills. We did everything we could to lower our tax bill (such as buy a ridiculously big house with an equally ridiculous mortgage), but still couldn't get our taxes below the "outrageous" level. Taxes were eating up nearly half of our combined salaries. We filed separately, and tried every investment/deduction avenue available, but it was clear we needed to do something else.

Every article, book and magazine we read told us that owning rental property was the number one option for people like us to shelter our income, reduce our taxes, and provide a stable investment. I fought and fought and fought, but Sandy and the Federal Government finally convinced me that we needed to explore this option. It didn't hurt that we had a good friend who was a realtor, had several rental properties, and was eager to teach us the ropes. And, he was so very positive about the experience. In a word, he lied.

I think it was February of 1992, right after we completed our taxes (and mailed all the big checks) that we said "enough is enough". You can only give the Feds so much of your hard earned money, and watch them piss it away before you decide to make a move. The search for rental property was on.

What Are You Thinking?

Our realtor friend had an interesting business model for his rental approach, and we decided to employ it, with a few minor twists. Our plan was to buy only single family homes and rent them out with option to buy. This is a rental agreement where a small portion of the rent is reserved as a down payment if the tenant would choose to buy the property. Our thought was that a lease/option approach would attract higher quality candidates, such as people who want to build equity, but cannot afford a home yet. Also, we figured that these people would treat the home as their own, as they would have an option to purchase it once the option money pot was large enough for the 5% down payment.

Nice theories, but this scenario never panned out. For all the houses we owned, and all the tenants living in them, not one family ever bought a house, even though many of them had accumulated more than enough down payment money sitting in the "option" accounts with us. Go figure.

Sandy and I had an additional altruistic goal that included giving people a hand up so that they could finally afford their first house. We set up our lease/option plan so that a tenant would have enough down payment money after 4-5 years. We never intended to own the home longer than that. Instead, we would own several houses at one time, and just keep "turning" them. We were going to make every "down and out" Clevelander into a homeowner before we were done. Yes, we can be very naïve. I submit that we had more heart than brains on this issue.

If you consider yourself a nice person, don't like conflict, and believe that human kind is generally honest and forthright, then just forget about this "business", please. If this sounds like you, then take our advice, and run screaming away from this harebrained idea. The money you spent for this book will turn out to be the best investment you will ever make in your life, trust me.

Look for our next book, which will be titled: "A Fool's Guide to Parenting"

Chapter 2

How to Buy Your First House?

Alright, so you just won't listen. If you're still reading, then you must be more committed to this idea than we thought. After all, we know you're not reading on because we are such captivating writers. We're engineers, after all. We're not supposed to have interesting personalities.

OK, on to house buying. There are several ways that you can approach this.

Believe it or not, the guy in the infomercial hawking his book about buying houses without any of your own money technically has a point. (You might want to know, however, that several of the people selling you information on how to prosper in the real estate game make their money by selling information to potential landlords and not by selling real estate.) You can do this, if you have a good credit record and have a few bucks in the bank to prove that you are a credible risk. I think they call this "collateral":-)

If you take this approach, you are essentially forfeiting any cash flow that you might be able to get from the rent, and are pursuing a longer term, capital investment basis. Cash flow is the money left over after the mortgage, interest, maintenance and taxes are paid. In other words, you will make your money when you sell the property, and the percent return should be quite astronomical, as you have put very little money (capital) into the house.

You need a good relationship with your bank to pull this off. We recommend finding a bank willing to work with you, and sell yourself as a serious investor with a "huge" future in this business. After we bought our "ridiculous" house to live in (with the ridiculous mortgage), we found it easy to expand our relationship with the bank, and managed to rate the services of a private banker. If you can do this, you will be much better off.

The private banker is usually someone fairly high up in the bank management chain, and this person can expedite real estate and banking transactions like nobody's business. As you foster this relationship, you will find that this person can make buying and selling homes a snap, with a fraction of the fees you would normally pay. If you must be a landlord, then for goodness sake, try to establish a relationship with the bank of your choice, and get a private banker to work with you.

A private banker will make it much easier for you to follow the home buying approach that requires very little (if any) money.

Here's how it works.

Our business model was to buy single family homes in the nice, safe West Park section of Cleveland. We tried to buy 3 bedroom houses only (although near the end, when we thought we were rental Gods, we bought some 2 bedroom homes which turned out to be big mistakes). In order to buy the home for no or little money down, you need to be able to buy the house for less than market value. This wasn't difficult for us, because we always chose homes that required a significant amount of "cosmetic" fix ups. This substantially undervalues a house.

So, look for houses that are dirty, badly wallpapered, dated, worn carpeting, in need of paint, etc. These are cosmetic problems that you can easily fix yourself at low costs, but most other house hunters are scared away from. Most people cannot tell the cosmetic problems from the real serious problems in the home that will cost a substantial amount of money to correct.

After you bid on the house and the bid gets accepted, your bank will want an appraisal of the house (among other things). Work with the appraiser and explain all of the work you will be doing to update the house, and show them the sales price of comparable houses in the same neighborhood that have sold for more than you paid for your house. (Your real estate agent can provide this sales information.)

The cost of an appraisal will vary from place to place. However, you should expect to pay about $300 for an appraisal on properties up to $300,000 and about $400 for properties between $300,000 and $500,000. If you get involved with apartment buildings, expect to pay $3000 for an appraisal on properties up to $300,000, $4000 for properties up to $1,000,000 and the prices should only increase slightly from there.

When appraising the home, the appraiser will likely ignore the cosmetic problems and give the house the value that it truly deserves now. You should be able to determine from the appraisal an approximate value of the property once it is fixed up. The loan to purchase the property is a commercial or business loan and the required down payment and interest rate are significantly higher than for a house you would purchase to live in. As you increase your portfolio of houses, the amount of debt (your debt load) increases and you become an increasing risk to the bank. You may find that your ability to obtain new loans at good interest rates may decrease as the number of properties you own increases.

Even still, most private bankers will allow you to borrow up to 90% of the appraised value of the home, at least for your first rental home. As you establish your relationship, you may be able to get even more than that.

If you have equity in your present home, you may be able to take out a home equity loan to purchase the initial property. After fixing the property up, have an appraisal performed then approach the bank for a loan. If your cosmetic improvements have increased the value of the property by enough to cover an acceptable down payment, you may be able to create a down payment out of your "sweat equity", the effort and investment you put into improving the home.

As an example of this method, let's say that you bid $80,000 for a single family home, but other comparable homes in the area are selling for $100,000. Let's say your appraiser thinks your home is not quite as nice (or as big) as the other comparable homes, so he appraises your home at $90,000.

If your banker loans you 90% of the appraised value, you will be approved for a loan of $81,000. Not only can you buy the house with "no money down", but will also be left with an extra $1000 to cover some of the closing costs. You may have to pony up another $1000-$2000 for closing costs, but you just bought a $90,000 for a very minimal sum.

Again, the down side of this approach is that your rent will likely go toward paying the mortgage, and there will be no cash flow. In some cases, the rent may not cover the whole mortgage, and you may be stuck with a small monthly bill to cover the difference. We wouldn't recommend going this far because negative cash flow is taboo in most business ventures that don't end in dot com. And look how far negative cash flow got those businesses.

A second approach, and one that we preferred, would be to put the traditional 20% down on the home. This leaves you with a much smaller mortgage, and allows you more flexibility to price the rent for the home. Also, this approach almost guarantees that you will have some small positive cash flow every month (assuming the tenant pays you each month). You can use this money to help pay your own bills, or save it up for the eventual rainy day maintenance that you will have with the home.

The downside of this approach is that you tie up some money in the house. For the example above, you would need 20% of $80,000, or $16,000 to buy the house plus closing costs. The return on investment will not be as high when you sell the property, as with the first approach outlined above. The other downside is that you need to have some money saved up to buy the house, and this will limit how many houses you can buy and rent (unless you are Donald Trump and even he was many millions of dollars in debt for a while).

A third approach would be to buy the house outright. The advantage of this approach is that you do not have to pay interest on a loan, and so your cash flow from the rental property is maximized. This can be a substantial cash infusion every month.

The downside of this approach is similar to the second approach in that you need money to buy a house outright. Again, it would also limit how many homes you could buy and you will be more likely to show taxable gains on the property.

How to Buy Your First House?

We used this approach for a couple of our houses, and being conservative engineers, we liked this approach quite a lot. While it tied up a lot of money, it did not expose us when tenants did not pay the rent or were late. We didn't have to come up with money to pay the mortgage because the tenant either was delinquent or skipped out on us.

So, you will probably be like us, and use a combination of these approaches as you acquire rental property. Properties may lend themselves better to one approach than another. Just remember that the "no money down" approach is the most risky, and someone will have to pay the bank. That someone may frequently be YOU, especially if your tenant turns out to be a nightmare, or you have to ask too much to rent the property and have trouble filling the vacancy.

Get informed about housing prices!!!

To help you avoid the trap of buying "too much house", make sure that you study the area that you want to own rental property, and find out what other people are paying for rent for similar properties.

This is easy to do, but will require some sleuthing on your part.

Sit down with the Sunday paper and a detailed map of your city. If your city has neighborhoods with names, this will be easy. For example, we could go to our local paper and look for houses for rent in the West Park area. Then, we could see where the houses were on the map, and make a note of the amenities and the rental price.

When we first started, we visited many of these properties (there are usually open houses), and pretended to be potential renters. We got a tour of the place, and many times, got ideas from the application form, etc. that we applied to our business. It sounds cold, but remember that these people are your competitors. You are all vying for the same, good tenants.

You should be able to get a good idea about what a house should go for (rental wise) depending on how many rooms it has, which street it is located on, etc. You then should do the math to figure out the maximum price you should pay for a house in that area, so that you don't buy a house that is so expensive you can't get the rent you need to pay the mortgage. Doing this homework is critical to the eventual success of the property and the decisions you make at this point are ones you endure through the entire time you own the place.

Our approach was to buy good quality houses, and update them entirely, so that they would look newer than many of the other rental properties. This allowed us to price the rent at the high end of the range. We found that this attracted better quality candidates.

You may want to choose another approach, such as keeping the rent as low as possible to attract the maximum number of candidates. This works too.

However, be aware that buying really poor houses and charging really low rent generally attracts all sorts of people that may not be reliable tenants. It may not be obvious, but your tenants are like your extended family. Their problems suddenly become your problems, even intensely personal things. Personal problems can often lead to problems paying the rent, and you will have to deal with this.

Just think of it this way. Would you want to do business with your in-laws? How about your loser buddies, or a financially challenged brother or sister? I didn't think so.

Advice. Buy good quality homes, fix them up to look brand new, and charge as high a rent as possible. Our experience is that there was a large market and higher quality tenants for homes such as these.

Repeat after me: Three Bedrooms

For some reason, three bedrooms seemed to be the magical number. Buy a two bedroom house at your own peril. We never had enough money to buy bigger houses, so I'm guessing that anything above three bedrooms is probably OK. Just make sure you can get enough rent to cover the mortgage.

We had better luck finding suitable tenants with three bedroom homes. The rent is higher, of course, and we think that more responsible people tend to realize that they need at least three bedrooms to raise their family. Our experience showed that two bedroom homes attracted much more desperate people. Of course, this is observational speculation. We have no hard science to back this up. But, in our market, I'd take this to the bank.

In other areas (especially high rent cities), you might find that this cut off lies in a different place. But, there does seem to be a relationship with housing space and quality candidates. Try to determine where this cut off lies for your market.

Our best recommendation for doing this is for you to use your common sense. In your market, what would be a reasonable space for a small family (husband, wife and two kids)? Don't buy anything that falls below this reasonable standard.

Hire an inspector!

In the beginning, you may not be an expert at inspecting the houses you want to buy. To be successful, you need to ensure that there are not significant problems with the home. These will always be hidden, so you need an expert to check this out for you.

All major appliances need to be checked out. The furnace, air conditioner, Jacuzzi (just kidding), etc. need to be examined.

Structural elements must be sound. The inspector will evaluate the basement, the walls, the electrical, the plumbing, the attic, the flooring, etc. This guy can save you a bundle, especially if there are major hidden problems in the home.

A good inspector costs about $200. He will take 2-4 hours inspecting the property, and provide you with a very detailed report. This written report should cover doors and windows, roofing, electrical, foundation, heating and cooling systems, insulation, plumbing and structural integrity. Wood boring insects, such as termites, carpenter ants and bees, may require a separate inspection. To find a good inspector, talk to everyone you know that has ever bought a house and used an inspector. Talk to real estate agents. Talk to everyone. See if you can locate a qualified inspector. If not, consult the yellow pages and take a shot.

If the inspector finds any major problems with the home, you have a decision to make. If the home is undervalued, you have some room to negotiate with the sellers. If it is something expensive, but straightforward, like the house needs a new furnace or water heater, you could try to negotiate a lower price for the house that takes these repairs into account. I wouldn't go too far down this road. If there are several major appliances that need replacement, I would walk away. If there is that much wrong with the home, you can be sure there is much more that is yet to be discovered. When submitting your offer to purchase a property, make sure to include contingencies that you can walk away from the deal if the financing or home inspection is not acceptable.

Also, if the inspector finds major structural damage, you should walk away. There is no way to ever tell how much it will cost to fix problems like a buckled basement wall, or a roof problem. Walk away.

Also, be sure that you won't need a new roof, siding, driveway or a garage in the near future. These things cost a lot of money, and do not add additional value to the home. Everyone expects a house to have a roof that keeps you dry. Everyone expects to have a driveway, garage and siding. The only way I would buy a house like this is if it was so undervalued that we could make these repairs and come out ahead. I doubt you'll ever find this situation.

More likely, you will find a situation whereby if you make the repairs, you would raise the value of the home by the amount you paid to make the repairs. Best case!!! Now, why in the world would you want to do that?

Save the money, save the hassle, and go buy something else.

Finally, you will find that you will become a pretty good inspector yourself, as time goes on. If you're like us, you will keep an eye on the inspector and try to understand what he is doing. Plus, you will be doing a lot of fix up work, and will gain experience with every aspect of housing maintenance. In time, you will be able to inspect homes for structural problems, and access the quality of the roof, driveway and major appliances. You will also become familiar with the local and national building codes. This worked well for us in later years.

Some day, you may want to become an inspector yourself. I'd rather do this, than become a landlord. Better hours, better pay, less hassle. Oops, looks like I let you on to our little secret. Don't tell anyone.

For more information on home inspections, look into the book "Managing Your Rental House For Increased Income" by Doreen Bierbrier. She has written an excellent chapter on house inspections that will help the "do-it-yourself" crowd. The website http://www.housedetective.com/ also has valuable information plus a searchable database of qualified inspectors.

Buying a HUD home

We wouldn't recommend buying a foreclosed HUD home as your first foray into the business, but you could certainly do this down the line, as you gain experience. Sometimes you can find a really good deal on a home that only has cosmetic issues.

 The biggest risk here is that you will likely be inspecting a home that has all of its major utilities turned off. So, you cannot walk around the home and turn on water spigots, electrical or gas appliances to see what works and what does not. Nothing will work. Instead, you run the risk of discovering big problems that you won't know about until you already hold the deed to the property, and all the utilities are turned on. We did this once, and made out OK. It was great fun trying to replace the electrical box during the Cleveland winter (it gets cold here) with no heat in the house. I don't think I would want to do this again, but hey, I'm not one who likes a lot of surprises. You may like to live a bit

A Fool's Guide to Landlording

more dangerously. Just be careful of the unknowns if you choose this route.

Chapter 3

The "Fix-Up"

If you're not real handy around the house, have no fear. You will become quite an expert at house maintenance and repair. If you have these skills, you will enjoy putting them to use.

When we started, we had a lot of common sense household skills, but not a lot of repair talent. We knew how to shut off the water if a leak sprung, or if a pipe or water line needed replacing. We could maintain the furnace and water heater, and re-light pilots, etc. Painting was a snap, and electrical wiring was a natural skill.

But, if you so much as put a doorknob through drywall, we would be flummoxed over what to do. The whole thought of building walls and repairing them was scary.

Not any more. We have no qualms about cutting right into a wall, when it is necessary. And we can repair so well that you would think the wall was perfect. Of course now we get the calls when our families have similar issues, but there are worse things in life than helping out your family.

The list of skills we honed is just plain too long to list. From this perspective, owning rental homes was a truly valuable experience. Just think. What a great place to learn home repair skills. All your mistakes are made elsewhere, not in your own home. Just kidding.

Cosmetic repairs, while time consuming, are relatively inexpensive, and make the place look brand new. This is why we so strongly recommend that you look for homes that are structurally and mechanical sound, but require loads of cosmetic repairs. This strategy ensures that you will get a good deal on the property, and will be able to "freshen it up" for a minimal cost.

A Fool's Guide to Landlording

This chapter gives you some pointers on what to look for, and how easy or hard the problems are to repair.

Painting

Let's start with an easy one. Painting. We like to paint, and frankly, we are quite good at it. So, we usually paint the entire inside of the house. Again, nothing spruces up a home like a fresh coat of paint. Also, the smell of a freshly painted room conjures similar feelings to the "new car smell" in a car on the showroom floor.

Above all, take the following two pieces of advice when it comes to painting.

1. Don't buy the cheap stuff!!! If you do, you will likely increase your painting time by 50%. The cheap stuff is thinner, doesn't spread as nicely and doesn't cover nearly as well. With good paint, two coats give a professional look, and occasionally, one coat will suffice. With cheap paint, plan on at least three coats to look spiffy.

2. Standardize on one color – probably white. But be aware there are literally hundreds of colors of white. White may be a pure white, but generally always has a small amount of tint of another color such as yellow, blue, gray, beige or pink. Whatever your favorites, a good tip would be standardize on one color (tint), finish and manufacturer of paint. Why? First, this gives the house a uniform, clean appearance. Second, touch up is a breeze, as you will likely have "left-over" paint, and it will be very easy to remember which color/tint was used in the house. If you choose this recommended route, another good tip is to buy the paint in the 5 gallon bucket size for maximum economics.

Paints come in a variety of finishes: flat, eggshell, satin and semi-gloss. Avoid flat paint (except for ceilings), as this will look dull, and will not clean up well. Use a "Satin" or "Eggshell" finish. If you can't find this type of finish, use a semi-gloss.

In our area, we use Sherwin Williams paints. We used so much during the years, we signed up to have a contractor's account at the store, and received discounts on our purchases. This saved a boatload of money. Plus, Sherwin Williams has great service, and the folks in the store are very knowledgeable. They will get you out of at least one jam, in some form or fashion. Plus, they will get you the right products to save you time.

In the beginning, we tried to paint our houses with a creative flair. We are engineers after all, so you know this had to go badly. The more we tried to make these small houses look cool and contemporary, the more we failed. Most people were polite, even when you could tell they hated the paint scheme.

Lesson learned. Use one brand and color of quality paint. Our favorite color is Zurich White, which is still available on request from Sherwin Williams but they have a wide variety of equally nice colors in the current palette. The finish is definitely white, but not at all bland. It looks fresh and clean.

Always latex if possible, never enamel. The enamel stinks horribly, and is difficult to clean up. The latex smells OK, and cleans up with water. If it is an old house with enamel paint, you will have to compromise by putting down a primer coating that is also enamel. Then, you can convert to a latex paint with the finish coating. Ask your paint store how to do this, if you've never done it.

If the wall is badly marked up (with crayons, pens, whatever), then make sure you invest in a primer coating. The store can tint your primer coating to match the final coating which will improve your coverage. The primer is thicker, and is designed to cover up marks. Try the Pro-Mar® product at Sherwin Williams. It works wonders. We also found Bullseye 1-2-3® to be an effective product.

If the wall was in bad shape you may still have to put two coats of regular paint over the primer. If the wall is in good shape, and the color is close to white (e.g. not neon blue or Metallica black), then you will probably not require a primer coating, and you can put the standard two coats over the top. If the wall is "bright", then you should use a primer coating.

Make sure to also buy good quality roller coverings and brushes. Be sure to buy the good masking tape, also. Just like "measure twice, cut once", you want to tape first, paint later. Don't cut corners on taping door jambs, window frames, woodwork, etc. Your finished product will look so much better than painting free hand. Plus, you can paint more quickly.

Another tip is to tape the ceiling, right where the wall and ceiling meet. This is a bite of a job, because you have to use a ladder, and tape upside down. But, you won't risk hitting the roller into the ceiling, and again, the finish will look perfect.

Do the painting first, never after the carpeting gets put down. This will let you get a little sloppy, and move more quickly.

Paint away.

Replacing Carpeting

Another easy task is carpeting. Most homes you look at will be in need of at least some carpeting, so look at this as an opportunity to spruce the home up. Besides, with most tenants, you will be replacing carpeting frequently. Tenants are notoriously hard on carpeting.

Unfortunately, carpeting is not cheap. It will likely be the most expensive cosmetic repair you will have to make. But, there are ways to reduce the cost.

First, ALWAYS tear up the old carpeting yourself. This is a relatively easy job, and you can easily cut up the carpeting into strips that the garbage people will take away. Yes, it is a dusty, dirty job, but well worth it. Most places charge $1-2 per square yard to remove the old carpeting and padding. This can add up to several hundred dollars saved if you are replacing a lot of carpeting.

By doing this yourself, you also can perform a massive clean up of the floor that probably hasn't been done in quite some time.

The "Fix-Up"

Be prepared, however, to find all sorts of nasty things under the carpeting. If there were ever animals in the home (especially cats), you will find a substantial amount of dander between the padding and the floor itself. It looks like white dust, but it's not. It won't hurt you, but will probably gross you out.

Besides the dander, there will be general dust and dirt and lord knows what down there. Get your broom and sweep it. Get the vacuum cleaner and sweep it, and sweep it and sweep it. It never all goes into the bag for some reason.

Then, get out the mop and mop the hell out of the floor. You'll be amazed how much better the house will smell once you are done. Don't skimp on the elbow grease here. A mixture of bleach and water does a nice cleaning job, but don't drip on any carpeting you are not replacing.

Take the opportunity to nail down squeaky floorboards, and do general repair work on the floor (unevenness, etc.).

One additional warning. Once you have torn up a really nasty bit of carpeting, you will find it impossible to ever lay on the floor of a stranger's home again. After seeing all the crap IN the carpeting and UNDER the padding, you will live in fear the rest of your life. Not to worry, though, because the same crap is in your home carpeting as well. No matter how well you think you keep house. It's the nature of the beast.

Lastly, unless you've done carpeting, and have the proper tools, ALWAYS pay to have the carpeting installed. Installers get about $3 a square yard to lay down the carpeting, and they are good. Usually, they work in a two man team, and these guys can blaze through a room in no time at all. They know what they are doing, and they have special tools to stretch the carpet so it looks perfect. I've even seen guys so good that they work alone. It takes longer, but it still looks expert.

Alternatively, if the base boards are slightly above the floor as they should be, you may be able to purchase carpeting with integral foam backing and with a steady hand, cut the carpet to fit. If you find you are continually replacing carpet in a house that turns over annually, you may find this to be a cost effective solution.

The house will glow with cleanliness and new carpet smell. Be sure to lay down a plastic path when conducting open houses so the "new house look" is not damaged.

Plumbing

Ewwww. This is my least favorite part. Thank goodness Sandy has such natural skill at this. I'm getting better, but there was a time where me and drain pipes were mortal enemies. No matter how hard I worked to seal a drain, it would spite me.

You've probably been there. Have you ever had a drain that you replaced the piping, checked for leaks and everything was perfect, only to find water dripping three days later? Didn't leak for three bloody days, then all of a sudden it decides to start dripping. Grrrrrr.

Sandy has the expert touch. She can hook up piping, seal it and get it perfect like nobody's business. She gets most of the plumbing jobs.

To be fair, however, I should mention that there have been the occasional drains that test her mettle as well. I have never heard such words out of her mouth, as when plumbing refuses to cooperate. My, my.

Use plastic, where possible, because it is more flexible and versatile. You can bend it "just a bit" to fit. Beware, however, of the really cheap crap, because they never go together "just right", and that's all the invitation water needs. Water will find a way to leak, given the opportunity. So buy the better quality stuff, and use pipe tape everywhere. Pipe dope is recommended for all places where a fixture or drain comes into contact with porcelain, plastic or metal. I'm referring to sinks, counters, etc.

Learn how to solder. You will, at some point, be replacing a fixture (such as a bathtub/shower assembly) where copper pipes will require "sweating" to remove and re-solder. You'll get the knack for this quickly.

When soldering, buy "lead-free" solder wire for safety. And don't spare the flux. Also, get ALL of the water out of the line, or you'll never get the joint hot enough to melt the solder and set it properly. Even a very small amount of water will prevent you from soldering the joint properly.

If you have a valve that lets in just a "teeny, tiny" bit of water, here is a trick. Stick a small piece of white bread inside the leaking pipe, and continue on as if the water flow has stopped completely. (Yes, it has to be white bread. Don't ask me, ask my Dad.) This should give you time to heat the joint and make the repair. Not to worry, the bread will saturate and get blown through the pipe once you turn the water back on. I'm assuming that you haven't shoved the whole loaf in there, of course.

To undo a fixture, attach vice grips on the fixture or the pipe a good six inches from the joint. Heat the crap out of the joint, until you see the old solder getting semi-liquid. You won't have but a moment, but when you see this, put down the torch, and rotate the pipe with the vice grips in an upward motion. The pipe should slide out of the joint. If not, start heating again.

If the vice grips are too close to the heat, you will burn your hand but good. Never grab the pipe with bare hands to remove. You'll do this only once in your life, trust me.

Before re-soldering, be sure to let the pipe cool and use steel wool to clean the old solder off. Get it squeaky clean, as this will ensure a good seal when you re-solder.

When re-soldering, rub flux all over the female joint/fixture and on the male end of the pipe. Apply liberally, as the flux will just melt away and be gone.

Put the joint together, and heat away. You'll hear the flux melting, and it will sound sort of like crackling. After about 30 seconds, the joint will be hot enough for soldering. With the torch in one hand, and the solder wire in the other, pull the heat off of the joint and start applying the solder. If the wire melts easily and begins flowing around the joint, you have the right temperature. If the wire won't melt, or is coming off in gobs, stop and continue heating. Try to do this in one fell swoop, as heating and re-heating while you are applying wire may not form the best seal.

Have a nice damp towel with you. After applying the solder wire, and you are confident that the seal is complete, touch the joint with the damp cloth (carefully, so as not to burn yourself). This will cool the joint quickly so the solder immediately sets up, and does not have a chance to separate from the joint due to gravity. Let it cool a bit, and test for leaks.

Toilets are easier to replace then they look. It's never fun to replace toilets for me because I have a hard time having my face so close to the scene of many a nasty bodily function for such a long period of time. It's just a visual thing, I guess.

If you have ever had the pleasure of removing a toilet, you know that the porcelain base sits over a pipe that connects to a hole in the floor. A wax ring is used to seal the two together and prevent water and what not from leaking out. Two threaded bolts with nuts keep the base in place. Sometimes getting these nuts off is an impossible task. A simple technique to use if the nuts are stuck is to liberally apply a "Liquid wrench" type product and let it sit. The next part requires two people. The "Wrencher" gets the nut un-stuck so it begins moving. The "Lifter" begins lifting the base so it stays firmly against the bottom of the nut to keep some tension. The "Wrencher" brings the nut toward the top of the threads (you'll need to be working alternatively on both bolts) and the "Lifter" keeps the system in tension. Eventually you should be able to get the base off the mount.

When replacing a toilet, always buy a new wax seal. They're dirt cheap, and save headaches. Besides, your old seal, no matter in how good of shape, has a memory. It is used to your old toilet, and will likely not conform perfectly to the new toilet, even if you buy exactly the same model. You don't want to have to take the toilet apart twice, so don't go cheap on me here. Buy the wax.

Electrical

Near and dear to my heart is the electrical repairs. I can't say why, but I really enjoy doing electrical work. I have a bit of a knack for it, and I like these types of problems because, unlike plumbing, the problem is either solved, or it is not. You won't get an outlet working, only to find it leaking electricity three days later.

Since we were buying houses 40 years old and older, there generally was quite a bit of electrical work to do. I usually tackled this first, while Sandy fixed any plumbing issues.

A simple tip. When planning your work schedule for the home, always perform the electrical work early in the day, before nightfall. This way, there will be light to work by, and you won't have to string up a work light just to see what you're doing. This may sound obvious, but it is easily forgotten. Once you pull the breaker, you will be amazed at how dark the world becomes.

One nice way to freshen up the house is to replace all of the wall outlets with nice fresh white new outlets. You can buy these in 10 packs very cheaply. Add the ground and some GFI's (Ground Fault Indicators), and bring your building up to code. This may be required in some geographic areas, or merely recommended in others.

Work room by room. Find the fuse or breaker that corresponds to the room you are working on, and pull it out, or turn it off. Never work with live electricity. Remember, especially in older homes, that the electricity may not be wired room by room. Always check the fixture and/or outlet you are working on has been turned off before beginning your electrical work.

We'd recommend buying an electrical testing device which allows you to determine exactly which fuse corresponds to which electrical outlet and fixture. You should be able to buy one of these for less than $20 in most areas.

Then, room by room, replace all of the wall outlets and any light switches. You will see quite a big difference in the room appearance, plus, you are ensuring that all of the outlets work and are properly grounded.

Sometimes, there are rooms that would be enhanced by having additional lighting or power outlets. I usually tackle these issues next. Again, remember to turn off the power to this section of the house first. Then, splice into one of the power lines in the room, and put in a junction box. Connect the desired power wire to the junction box, and run the line to the desired location. If you don't feel confident working with electricity, prepare a written plan of what you would like and contract with a licensed electrician.

For installing two-way or three-way switches, we recommend that you get yourself a simple electrical "how to" manual. You should find the instructions very simple.

Although I could probably tackle it, I usually stayed away from any problems within the main electrical box itself. After seeing a professional install a new one for me at the HUD house (described later), I was convinced that this was over my head. There is just a bee's nest of wires in the box. My advice, call a professional, and get several quotes. The lowest quote is not always the best, so beware of an electrician who's quote is significantly below the others. Also, if this electrician is available immediately, you should be concerned.

It may be that this particular electrician is not very good, and this explains why he doesn't have any work. This is not always true, but something to watch out for.

Indoor wiring should use indoor ROMAX wires (white). Outdoor wiring should use the outdoor ROMAX (gray). That's about all there is to electrical issues.

Flooring

We never installed any tile flooring, but we did plenty of vinyl and linoleum floors. Vinyl flooring typically comes in the 9-12" square variety, while linoleum comes in rolls, like carpeting.

The "Fix-Up"

Linoleum gives a cleaner look (no seams), but we found this much harder to put down. Especially in rooms with many obstacles that must be cut around. Personally, we liked the vinyl squares.

In houses such as we bought, only the kitchen and bathrooms were not carpeted. In general, we would replace the flooring in both rooms. Again, this makes for a nice, clean and fresh look in the home.

If the current flooring is nice and flat, without ridges in the current vinyl tile, you can lay down a new flooring right over the top. If there are some problem areas where pieces of the tile are broken away, you can use "mastic" to fix the problem. Mastic is a plaster type material that can be laid down and smoothed over the uneven parts. It dries hard and smooth. Be sure to smooth the material as much as possible before drying. Even the most minimal ridge will show through the vinyl floor tiles, as the tiles themselves are often very thin.

At your local hardware store, you will find a large choice of tiles to choose from, and they are fairly inexpensive. Measure the room, or count the current tiles, to determine how many you will need. Laying the tile is a snap, so don't be scared away if you've never done this.

Look at how the current tile was laid down, and decide if this is how you want your room to look with the new tile. Many times, we found that we didn't like the way the pattern was laid down. So, we would choose the wall we wanted to begin with a full tile, and began here.

The only tools you will need are a ruler/measuring tape, scissors and/or carpet cutters (box cutters). We liked to work with scissors, as box cutters can sometimes be dangerous to your fingers.

Here is a little tip you will really appreciate. While you are working from your starting position, take several tiles and place them in the oven. Put the oven on its lowest setting.

A Fool's Guide to Landlording

Then, when you get to any of the other walls in the house, or have to work around an obstacle, such as a toilet, sink or other fixture, use one of the warm tiles to cut to dimension. You will find that the warm thin tiles cut much easier, and will be much easier to mold into place. Also, if there is a small imperfection in the floor (such as a small bump), a warm tile will conform to the floor perfectly. Much better than a plain old cold tile.

You will be doing a lot of cutting. Keep rotating in new tiles into the oven to ensure you always have a warm one to cut.

Also, be very careful with the bits that you cut from the tiles. Don't just scatter them about the unfinished floor. Even the tiniest little piece of cut tile will cause an imperfection in the final flooring if you just cover over it with a new tile. Because these tiles are thin, there will be a little bump wherever there is a little piece trapped below the tile. This is harder than it sounds. Do the best that you can.

The tiles are self adhesive, so you will be able to place the tile where you want it, and even move it a bit if you don't have it situated perfectly the first time.

Be sure to buy some floor glue. If you find that the tiles are not sticking as well as you would like, then put down a small amount of floor glue, and put the tile down over the glue. A small amount goes a long way, and the extra will come seeping up through the seams. When using floor glue, have a damp towel handy to continually wipe up any glue that seeps through. Don't let it dry, or it will be a bear to remove.

If you get in trouble here, just wait for the glue to dry completely, and remove with a petroleum product, such as paint thinner. Dampen a towel with the thinner, and use as sparingly as possible. Using large amounts or sloshing it around can damage the look of the vinyl tile. Keep the extra tiles in the box and label with the house address, room location and date. Don't keep these at the rental property, keep them in your maintenance area for later repairs.

With linoleum, you will have to use floor glue. If you absolutely have to have linoleum, then use cardboard or another material to create a template of the pattern you want to make in a room. Lie out the linoleum in another room, put the template on top, and cut to size. Then, spread glue all over the floor to be covered, and begin to lay the linoleum down little by little. This is not fun at all, unless the room has no obstacles.

Finally, if the floor is really badly damaged, or there are too many layers already laid down, be sure to rip up the old floor. This is hard work, normally. Just keep chipping away. If you contract the new flooring to be installed, they may just add a new layer of Luan flooring (basically very thin plywood) over the existing tiles and put the new flooring on top.

Take it down to the plywood. Sand any areas that need to be flattened. Then, buy some Luan board, cut it, and lay it down as the foundation for the vinyl tiles. Luan board is a very thin (and light) wood that creates a wonderfully flat surface to lay tiles onto. If you go this route, your floor should come out perfectly flat.

Nice Touches

In all of our houses, we would replace most of the ceiling light fixtures, after we painted the ceilings. Again, even when you buy inexpensive fixtures, this makes the house; look so new and fresh. The electrical bit is easy, but again, be sure to turn off the power.

Another nice touch is to put a ceiling fan in any room that already has an overhead light. Nearly all of the bedrooms will have an overhead light with a wall switch. This makes it easy to install a fan, which is a very nice and inexpensive amenity.

You can buy ceiling fans with light fixtures very cheaply. Put one in each bedroom and the kitchen, at a minimum. Installing a fan is quite easy, once you have the knack. Today's fans are designed to self support themselves while you do the wiring. Just be sure to read the instructions, as the order of installation is crucial. It is possible to get it fully installed, and then realize that you forgot to put the ceiling shroud on, which will require you to completely disassemble all of your work.

You could power the fan two ways. The easy way is to just use the switch to power both the fan and the lights as one unit. If you do this, then the fan will operate with a pull string.

Another way with some pizzazz is to buy a special switch which will allow the fan to be operated at the switch, as well as the light. There are several types of switches, but all of them will have one control for the lights and one for the fan. I like the switches that allow for dimming of the lights, and variable control of the fan. You may not want to get this fancy.

There are many nice upgrades you can easily make, but I'll mention just one more. Weather stripping.

We would recommend that you buy some weather stripping, and redo all of the doors in the home. You will be surprised at how much difference this makes. You will cut down the draft significantly. Additionally, you could re-caulk the windows for even more effect. This will save your tenant on utility bills throughout the year, and make the home more comfortable. A happy tenant is a paying tenant.

Major Repairs

If major repairs are required, we would hire a contractor. Major repairs include furnaces, hot water tanks, dishwashers, roofs, driveway repairs, etc. Our advice would be to find a reputable HVAC contractor, and use them exclusively. If you go cheap here, you will get cheap. We like to do it once, and do it right. Remember the following truism – "A good contractor will cost you a lot, a bad contractor will cost you a lot more."

A good repairman can cost a lot. But, a botched "do-it-yourself" can cost twice as much. Plus, you'll have to put up with the repairman's giggles when you bring him in to fix your mess. He may even charge you more because he'll feel you are desperate and have no alternative.

The "Fix-Up"

Plus, a good quality HVAC company will begin to reward you as you provide a steady stream of business. After a few jobs, the HVAC company generally will give you very competitive bids, and throw in a few extra, nice to haves, that you will really appreciate.

When we replaced the furnace in one house (see The Losers horror story), the contractor did such beautiful work. We thought we were entering the Taj Mahal when we stepped in the door to inspect the work. I never thought a furnace assembly could look so beautiful.

Other rewards include prompt service and follow up. If you are not satisfied with any aspect of the job (or something doesn't work right), they will be right there to correct the problem. You will never hear again from a fly-by-night company.

If you haven't already, you'll likely learn some of these skills. Why? Take a look at the average cost per hour of hiring a professional.

The following Table gives examples of an average cost of labor for some of the major trade professionals.

Profession	Average Hourly Rate (in US Dollars)
Brick Layer	33.05
Carpenter	47.85
Dry wall Installer	41.10
Electrician	45.40
Painter	42.02
Pipe fitter (Plumber)	47.91

Source: 2003 National Construction Estimator, 51st Edition, Craftsman Book Company, edited by Dave Ogershok, 2002.

These rates vary extensively based upon geographic region. New York City and Alaska would easily see rates 50% higher than these. Texas, South Carolina and Alabama would see rates about

15% lower. This does not include the services of a helper who's pay is about 2/3rds of that listed for each profession. Local Union rates also significantly influence pricing. This rate will be charged for travel time as well as time at your site and may include a set-up or minimum charge.

Pay for a few repairs, and you'll soon be very motivated to learn to do some of these things yourself.

In Conclusion

These are just some of the most common repairs you can be expected to perform. Having a partner helps significantly. You both will have different strengths, and you can split the work up depending on these strengths.

When Sandy and I would begin work on a house, she would go right to the plumbing, and I right to the electrical. We then painted and did most other things together. Also, you'll be surprised how often the extra set of hands makes impossible jobs possible.

Go it alone at your own risk, here. My real estate friend often was alone to do repair work and he was a very unhappy man.

Chapter 4

Finding the "Ideal" Tenant

There is no "Ideal" tenant, I'm sorry to say. But, you can find "good" tenants. The search is hard, and there is always a risk (as evidenced by the horror stores to follow), but you can get lucky if you have a system. Here is our system, and some interesting things you will learn about people along the way. Be prepared to be surprised. Your respect for humankind may be altered, negatively.

Create a one page application form. Use two pages, if you must, but one page is less likely to scare away potential applicants. The best way to do this is to use your common sense, and think of all the things you want to know about people you are about to enter a financial relationship with.

There are several good books on rental application forms. Go to the library and get a couple for additional ideas. Also, visit a few open houses for rental properties and make some mental notes on what other people are asking for on their applications. With these three sources, you will be able to construct a very nice form.

For your reference, the application form that we came up with is located in Appendix 1. Feel free to use this information at your will. However, if you use a credit verification agency, which we highly recommend you do, they will likely want you to use their form.

Many landlords charge a rental application fee. We always thought this was silly, and never did this ourselves. You may scare away some potential tenants, one of which might have been the "ideal" tenant. I just don't understand the philosophy here. It just doesn't make sense to trade potential tenants for the minimal amount of money you will make from the application fee. After all, your goal is to find a highly qualified, stable, responsible tenant who will uphold their end of the bargain. This will make you more money in the end.

Do what you like, but we wouldn't recommend charging an application fee.

Some of the best advice we got was to look inside the applicant's car for clues about the character of the person. This was very effective. After the people fill out the application form, see them to their car to say goodbye and good luck. This will enable you to take a look inside.

Generally, the condition of the inside of the car will reflect this person's nature. Is it a total mess, with things scattered all about? If so, what makes you think that this person will treat your house any differently? Perhaps the car doesn't need to be pristine, but it should be somewhat tidy.

If small children are involved, be a little more lenient. From our experience, there is no way to keep your car pristine with little ones. You just can't keep up with all of the food flying around in the back seat. Remember these are the same children that will be living in your house.

Place the Advertisement and Set Up the Open Houses

Once you have the house fixed up and the rental forms prepared, you are now ready to receive potential applicants. Again, look in your local Sunday newspaper in the housing rental section. Take a look at all of the various ads, and put together your own ad that uses the bits you like from the others. Add your own words, if you have special things you want to say.

Make yours a little bit longer and "fluffier" than the rest, and you'll get noticed. Run the ad for two consecutive weeks, and put times in there for two separate open houses on consecutive Sundays. We found Sundays to be the best.

Also, be sure to put a sign out on the front lawn indicating that the property is for rent. Make sure that a phone number can be

Finding the "Ideal" Tenant

seen plainly by people driving by. You will be surprised how many people respond to a lawn sign. This will ensure that you attract candidates who are familiar with the area, and have a desire to live in your neighborhood.

You may choose to only use a lawn sign, and not advertise broadly in a local newspaper. This will reduce the number of tenant applications, but may result in quickly finding potential tenants who are familiar with the area, and truly want to live in the house.

If you are in a football crazy town, like us, then be cognizant of conflict with football games. This will inevitably happen, but just be aware of it. You may find that the lady of the house is out shopping for a rental unit, while the man of the house is at home watching football. If the tenant has appeal, and makes the final cut, you will have the opportunity to meet the man at a later date.

Ideally, however, it would be nice to meet them both so that this can factor into your screening process. Many women come across very well, but when you meet the "lord of the house", well you can be quite turned off. Good responsible, handy men make good tenants. Look for these types of people.

The open house should run from about noon to 4pm. You will be exhausted after four hours of talking to people and helping them fill out forms. After two sessions, you should have plenty of people to choose from.

Expect to pay about $40-50 for the ad.

Meeting and Greetings

The hours you will spend during the open houses may be some of the most fascinating hours of your life. You will meet some of the most interesting people you have ever met, unless you regularly deal with the public.

People love to talk. They will tell you way more about their lives than you care to hear. But, you want to listen. Be a good listener, even if you are the kind of person that finds this painful.

They will share the most intimate details of their life with you. Take the time to listen to what they have to say, and ask leading questions that ensure that they will continue to divulge their true personalities.

Keep in mind that you are evaluating them. So ask questions that will inform you of their financial situations, their ability to maintain a home, their beliefs regarding issues of responsibility. You will have to sort through the chaff, but you will get a pretty good picture of the person in the meantime.

The best way to do this is to give a tour of the house, followed by an encounter where you fill out the application form together. Help them fill out the form and listen carefully to the questions they ask while filling out the form. This will tell you all you need to know.

Here is another great tip. The minute the prospective tenant leaves the premises, turn the application form over and make some hand written notes. If you work with a partner, it is best if both of you meet the applicants, so that you can both discuss your impressions. Many times, one of you will see something that the other has missed.

You will be taking so many applications that you will forget exactly what these folks looked like, and the details of your discussions. Make simple notes that will remind you about the details, and give your impressions of the suitability of these applicants as tenants.

Granted, this will be a subjective analysis, but when used together with the grading system described below, you will find this to be valuable information. Be sure to consult with your local laws and regulations regarding tenant selection, with particular emphasis on discrimination. You want to be fully informed in this area.

Now, let me give you some examples, then share some of the most interesting trends that we experienced.

Income

Income comes in all forms, and you will likely see every known form.

The best and easiest information to deal with will involve W2 information. This is the wage information from conventional employment, and this information will be accurate, as long as the individual in question still holds the said job.

This information can be verified through a credit reporting agency or by requesting recent pay stubs. Also, do not be ashamed to ask for the phone number of current employers and making calls to verify income and employment.

Employers are not required to provide income information, but they will generally verify employment. By requesting this information from your prospective tenant, you will usually find out, by default, if this person is telling the truth.

Strings of excuses, but no employer phone number, should raise a big, red flag. Be sure to push this issue. Information and phone numbers quickly given should give you confidence of the honesty of the individual. Check anyway.

Self employment income is another form of income. This one is difficult to evaluate, and we generally would talk at great length about the business, and try to get the prospective tenant to provide some financial information. Use credit reports and any financial information, such as bank records, that the applicant is willing to provide. Make it clear that income will be a large factor in determining if a tenant has suitable income to afford the rent. You may be surprised how much information a legitimate business person will provide to get the house. Self employed people are used to having to provide substantiation of their income.

A surprisingly large number of prospective tenants receive "under the table" income. Even those with "regular" jobs and W2's. Remember, you are not employed by the IRS, and your job is to determine the validity and stability of this income. Apply the same rules that you would for a normal W2 situation. Ask for deposit check information, and call employers for verification of employment.

Most, if not all, people also make substantial income that is "off the books", or "under the table". I am still amazed what a large underground economy that we have.

Often times, people will actually list this income on the application form, and will give you great detail as to how this money is earned. I'm sure the IRS would love to have this information, but this is not your concern. You are trying to find a tenant that is responsible enough to pay the rent, not solve all of the problems of society.

Many of the people who filed applications for our properties receive government subsidies in the form of child support, food stamps, Social Security or Aid to Dependant Children.

It was not unusual to be discussing a rental form with a prospective tenant, when one of the other adults would ask you to step outside to discuss a personal topic. Generally, this would involve an unmarried couple who were staying unmarried for financial reasons.

As an example, I can recall several times where, during the interview and review of the application form, I was asked to "step outside". Not to fight, mind you, rather, the individual wished to share "confidential information". In most cases, this involved a detailed explanation of how the prospective tenant received various forms of government support that would help pay the rent, but which could not be disclosed on paper for risk of being found out by the government.

For example, the most common "confidential information" consisted of the woman of the house receiving some form of government support, and should it be known that she was either married and/or living with a man, she would risk termination of payment. Therefore, the point of the meeting was to relay to me an additional income source that was purposely not listed on the form, due to concerns that the government would find out.

Finding the "Ideal" Tenant

Somehow, people like this thought that this would help make their case to me. In fact, we were not interested in leasing to people who were cheating the system. This didn't seem like a desirable character trait to have in a tenant, and we passed on many people for this reason alone.

One classic example that comes to mind involving a lady and her three crazed children. She made a special appointment with me one evening to fill out the application form. They arrived in a fury. It took us over an hour to fill out the application form, not because it was a difficult form to fill out, but because we had to continually get up and chase down a catastrophe in one of the rooms. The children were just plain wild and she had no control over them. During the course of the hour, I learned that she was receiving government subsidies for the older two of $300 per month each and was just about to get the younger one on the same program. She planned to use the money from the first two to pay the rent. How charming. After an hour, I literally had to throw them out of my house. They had torn down the blinds in several rooms, and caused various minor damage to each of the other rooms. I spent the next several hours cleaning up the mess. I don't think I need to say more.

Income should be the leading factor when establishing the quality of the candidate. You must ensure that your prospective tenant has the financial resources available to make the rent payments and have enough left over to meet basic needs. While this may seem obvious, it is not obvious to many applicants.

We had so many applications where it would be impossible for a particular family to live in our house and even make the rent payments. You would think that people would have figured exactly how much rent they could actually pay, and search for housing that they could afford. Our experience indicates that many people do not take the time to make this simple calculation, or want more than they can afford.

A Fool's Guide to Landlording

"Debt"

Debt is bad!!! Any debt is bad.

OK, this is not realistic, but the truth is, you want to be their first, and only, debtor. If they owe other people money, especially official institutions, you will be low on the debtor "pecking order".

People are pretty honest about these things, believe it or not, and they will generally spend a considerable amount of time talking about their debt loads.

The people with low debt loads will usually question you as to why you need this info. When convinced, they will provide a terse description and value. The people with humongous debt loads, will try to explain it away before putting it on paper.

If you conversation goes on past 10 minutes on debt load, and they haven't filled the number in yet, you can be sure that the number they DO put in the box will be a low number. Count on the fact that their actual debt load is considerably higher.

So, look for folks with low debt loads. Regardless of the joke above, some debt is quite normal, and you will rarely find someone with zero debt. However, you should be able to quickly calculate an income to debt ratio to understand whether someone is overloaded with debt or not.

If you're going to buy a house, lending institutions don't like to see more than 36% of your gross monthly income going to debt. Of this, they feel about 28% should go toward housing. That only leaves 8% for other debts -- including a car payment, credit card debts, student loans and outstanding medical bills.

For example, if your prospective tenant makes $60,000 a year, the monthly gross pay is $5,000. Okay, so 36 percent of $5000 is $1800. The maximum housing payment would be 28 percent of the $5000, or $1400 with $400 available for car payments and other loans. For a prospective tenant making $25,000 per year, consider that the monthly gross pay is $2083, 36 percent (total

Finding the "Ideal" Tenant

debt level) is $750 and 28 percent (housing) is about $580 with $170 to cover other debts.

Why do you care? Credit card debt levels in the United States, and throughout the world, are soaring. Well, if they owe everybody and their brother money, what are the odds that you are high up the pecking order for payment? You are not as good at collecting money as are banks and others who are used to using legal procedures to get their money, and their filing bankruptcy is always a possibility.

Your only weapon is eviction, and after you read Chapter 6, you'll see that this weapon takes awhile to fire. They can stretch you out, while they pay everyone else. So, debt load factors in heavily.

"Handy-Man"

Another important attribute that we looked for in prospective tenants was their ability to maintain a house. Can they do simple things, like turn off a water valve if there is a leak in the house? Can they light the pilot light on a water heater should it blow out? Can they cut grass? Can and will they perform the simple, daily maintenance?

This is important for several reasons, the first of which is safety. As The Losers taught us from the horror stories, people without any basic knowledge of home ownership maintenance are a safety risk to themselves and to the house itself.

In addition, you don't want to be called out every other day, at all hours of the day, to be fixing ridiculously minor issues, such as changing a light bulb, etc. They should be expected to do this, especially in a lease with option to buy scenario.

If you are renting individual homes, the maintenance is not like an apartment building with an on-site maintenance person. This needs to be made clear up front. Most people who were looking to rent a house, especially a lease/option deal, completely understood this. The Losers were the only tenants we ever had an issue with in this area. So, at least we chose well in this area.

Stability

Could we think of a more nebulous topic to lay on you? Probably not. Yet, if you can quantify this, you will be more successful than most.

Our experience has proven to us that stable people make very good tenants. What do we mean by stable?

Well, look over our lease application in Appendix 1.

Note that we ask for lengths of time, as well as information. We want to know where you lived previously, AND we want to know how long you lived there. We want to know where you work, AND we want to know how long you worked there.

Stability. Are you a person who jumps from job to job? If so, isn't it plausible that you have some commitment issues, and most important, will go through spells where you are jobless, and unable to pay the rent.

Do you jump from residence to residence? Why? People don't usually do this willingly. Are you not able to get along with a landlord? Are you not paying your rent? What is going on?

If you have an application that shows frequent job movement and frequent residence movement, you should seriously question the stability of this person. This is a bad trend, and without reasonable explanation, would be enough to scare us away.

That's not to say that you can't be flexible. If you see recent movement (been in a job and or residence for just a short while), then question it and see what the reasons might be. Many times, people have a very plausible reason for a recent move, and it can be clear that this was a one time thing, or a special circumstance.

We would still grade them a bit lower on stability, but it wouldn't be a show stopper, like the "fly-by-nighter".

Other Stuff

Some of the general information includes a couple of important questions that will likely never be answered truthfully. The first; "Are you interested in the option of leasing this house to own it?" Make it clear that you are looking for tenants that want to be in for the long haul (and eventually purchase the home), and you will be sure to always get a "yes" answer for this box. People don't care, they will tell you whatever you want to hear just to make sure they are considered for the home.

The second question is: "Have you been evicted before?". Think anyone will ever answer yes??? In the old days (1990's), you generally had to take their word for this. Now, you can go to several web sites (see Chapter 8) and find out if these people have ever been evicted. If so, it doesn't matter the reason, strike them from your list of potential tenants. Cold, yes, but prudent.

Now, you may laugh and say, "Why are you asking these questions if you already know the answer?" Well, for one, there are some people that are really interested in the option route, and we want to hear what they have to say about this. We WANT to know who these people are.

But, most important, if they are not truthful on their form, then this can come back to haunt them at a later date. We had this with The Losers (Chapter 9), where they lied about the lease/option question. They were horrible tenants, and in the middle of our 100th tense meeting, they divulged that they never intended to buy the house.

I had wanted them to move on, but they held the upper hand. Once they told me how they had lied, I was able to turn this around on them. Fact is, I could've begun eviction procedures against them for lying on their application. It is in the lease, and besides, it is a common legal argument that I could've easily won.

I didn't go this far, but I did make the threat that they better back off because I had recourse if they didn't. Believe me, it helped the situation, and made it easier for us to get through the next few months until the lease ended. People become quite humble when you catch then in a flat out lie. It didn't hurt that I was really pissed off, and expressed these sentiments with them, either.

Pets

Don't do it. We did and we regret it.

When researching your market for rental property and market rental prices, you will notice the vast majority of landlords who clearly state "No Pets". We liked animals, and both had been around cats and dogs our whole lives. We thought that the landlords were being selfish, and thought we could create a marketing advantage by allowing pets. We would just charge $25 more a month for pets.

Our thinking was that there were lots of good, prospective tenants floating around because they were being turned away by the "No Pets" properties. This may be true, who knows.

It doesn't matter. In general, people don't take care of their pets, and the animals do more damage to your house than you can imagine. Don't listen to the owner. Every single person that had a pet said the same thing. "He/she is an angel. Never barks, never chews, blah, blah, blah". Bull. According to the owners, the animal never craps or pees either.

Lies, all lies. Most behaved as badly as their owners, and as I said, caused more damage to our homes than any other single thing.

Let me apologize to all you animal lovers out there, but this has to be said. Animals stink!!! Oh yes, it's true. For all of the houses we have been in to look at buying, and all of the homes we rented, you could tell the instant you walked in whether there was an animal living there or not.

And, you cannot fully get this smell out of the house, try as you might. Between the smell, the dander and the damage, trust us, enforce a "no pets" policy.

By the way, you will have tenants trying to sneak a pet in. Eventually, you will see it. Threaten eviction if they won't get rid of the animal. If you use any compassion at all, you will find more animals living in the house over the next few months. We know because it happened to us every time.

Intangibles

The intangibles are the notes that you made on the back of the form for each prospective tenant. This is not an exact science, but is a nice way to balance the specific items above with a bit of humanity.

The grade for the intangibles should be based on very human aspects, such as, did you like the people, could you get along well with these people, are they respectful, did they seem to like the house, or were they overly critical, etc.

In many cases, we would have several people with similar grades in the tangible category. When this happened, we would use the intangible grade to determine who we thought we could get along with best. After all, never forget that this is a relationship, and getting along will make life much easier for both of you.

Finally, you will find the rare individual that grades very high on the tangible issues, but has a zero on the intangibles. In most cases, this simply means that you couldn't stand to be around this person, or just did not like their behavior in the least. You will need to have a working relationship with your tenants and you will need to get along. Imagine, if during a storm, part of the roof blows off and damages your tenant's belongings along with the damage to your property. Is this someone you would be able to work through a bad situation with? Do you really want this person in your life?

A Fool's Guide to Landlording

Ratings Table

Great!! Now you've got an idea of what to look for, but are wondering how you actually put all the grades together to determine a winner. Again, there is no wrong way to do this, and all we are offering is our suggestions and our methods. You will want to customize this to your own personal preferences.

We used a simple table to grade our candidates. An example of the table is shown below.

Tenant Number	Income	Debt	Abilities	Stability	Other	Intangibles	Total
Tenant 1	3	1	5	2	1	3	15
Tenant 2	5	3	2	2	2	4	18
Tenant 3	5	4	4	4	3	4	24
Tenant 4	4	5	5	5	4	4	27
Tenant 5	2	3	4	3	3	3	18
Tenant 6	3	3	3	3	3	3	18

We used the grading scale of 0 to 5, with 0 being the worst and 5 being the best.

Remember, all of these prospective tenants have sufficient income to pay the rent, or they would not have even made this list. The grading in the income column is simply our evaluation of how tight the finances will be in this household. So the income column is intended to factor in income minus the debts. If this value drops below 3, in our grading system, then there is cause for concern. More on this later.

Now, the total appears in the far right column, and most of the time, the scores are very close for the first half dozen candidates.

Finding the "Ideal" Tenant

The first thing we would do is reorganize the table, and sort it to put the best candidate on the top, and the worst on the bottom, as shown in the next table.

Tenant Number	Income	Debt	Abilities	Stability	Other	Intangibles	Total
Tenant 4	4	5	5	5	4	4	27
Tenant 3	5	4	4	4	3	4	24
Tenant 2	5	3	2	2	2	4	18
Tenant 5	2	3	4	3	3	3	18
Tenant 6	3	3	3	3	3	3	18
Tenant 1	3	1	5	2	1	3	15

Tenant 4 is at the top with a score of 27. Next is Tenant 3 with 24, and then three candidates tied with 18. This is pretty normal, and you will have many candidates tied with the same score.

Selecting the Tenant

The next step in our process was to down select to the top three candidates. Why three? Because often times the number one candidate may have already taken another place. Remember, this is a competitive market, and everyone wants the best people to occupy their properties. If these folks scored high on our list, then they probably scored high on every other rental application that they filled out.

Notice in our example above, it is not immediately clear who the third candidate should be, as there are three people tied for third place. We would take a hard look at the grades of these three candidates, and pay special attention to the intangibles. In this particular case, we would select Tenant 2 as our third candidate because of the strong income and intangibles scores.

After you've been in this for some time, you can tell a really outstanding candidate. If this happens, circumvent the process and immediately call these people and ask if they are still interested in renting the property. If they are, pull the credit report, get together as soon as possible and sign the lease.

Other landlords may do this to you, and you're number one candidate may have already been snared. Be prepared for this eventuality.

So, now, you have down selected to three potential candidates. Stop right now, and get on the Internet. There are several outstanding sites that can help you determine the quality of individual prospective tenants. Chapter 8 goes into Internet sites in more detail, but here is the synopsis.

You want to find out if the candidates have a poor credit record and if they have ever been evicted. For the credit record information, you have many choices. You can either use a website like the National Association of Independent Landlords (http://www.nail-usa.com/), or you can use "old fashion" sources such as Experion, TransUnion or Equifax, whose phone numbers can be found in the Yellow Pages. Expect to pay between $10 and $25 per candidate.

There are also many useful Web sites that you could visit to conduct tenant screening. We'd recommend agoodtenant.com for their screening services.

The results from these searches should be factored into your point system above. Also, if the results come back good on one or all of the candidates, this should give you some security that you are making a good choice. Let's assume all is well, and your top candidates remain in the order shown above.

Call the top candidate and see if they are still interested. If they are, set up a meeting immediately. Call the number two and number three tenants, congratulate them on being in the top three, and let them know that they are not yet out of the running.

This may seem a little odd to you, but people love to hear that they did well on this test of life. In all cases, people were so happy to find out that they made the top three, that they just glowed. And, it is true that they are still in the running, as nothing is final until the paperwork is signed. By making this simple phone call, and promising to let them know the final outcome very soon, you will have these folks waiting and wishing you to call back to give them good news.

If the number one candidate meets with you again, and signs the lease, then call number two and three and politely tell them that number one has signed. Express your gratitude for their interest, and your sorrow for not being able to accommodate their wishes. You will have made them proud of themselves, and they will actually thank you taking the time to make the calls.

So many applicants told us that they appreciated the phone calls, even when they were rejected. Apparently, many landlords do not even bother to call after the initial visit. Anyway, if the number one applicant changes their mind, then work your way down to number two, and eventually number three if necessary.

If all three do not work out, then take a look at the other scores, and determine if a fourth or fifth candidate will work. Often times they will not qualify, and you will have to start over again by placing an ad and taking applications.

At this point, be sure to call everyone who has applied and tell them that you are sorry, but they did not make the cut. Be polite and apologetic. No one likes to get this type of phone call. But, you can show a little humanity with a small white lie. Tell everyone that they scored in the upper third percentile.

"You did really well and made it in the top third of candidates. But, I'm so sorry, there were so many qualified applicants, and one of the folks in front of you has agreed to rent the property. We've just signed the lease, and I wanted to let you know as soon as possible. Thank you for your interest in our home, and we wish you the best of luck in finding a nice place to live."

A Fool's Guide to Landlording

Corny, maybe. Most of it is true, and we didn't see the point of insulting people who scored poorly. We figured that they had enough problems, and probably didn't get positive messages often. Again, you'd be surprised how much this brightened someone's day.

On the other hand, DO NOT fall into desperation and take a candidate that is not suitable just because you do not want to start the process again. It is better to lose a few weeks of rent payment up front while searching for more qualified tenants, than to take the easy route and sign up someone who is not qualified. You will pay for this decision down the road.

You should be in a solid financial position yourself so you don't have to take any candidate just because there is an additional mortgage to pay.

The problems you encounter will compound with time, and you'll either be stuck with lousy tenants for a year or longer, or you will be learning about eviction. Either way, you'll stand to lose a lot of money and sanity in the process. We did this once, and we learned our lesson quite well. For a refresher, see the horror story on The Druggies.

If you are in this situation, take a deep breath, and resubmit the ad. As difficult as this is to do, trust us, this is very good advice.

For more good advice on selecting tenants, get the books "Landlording" by Leigh Robinson and "Managing Your Rental House For Increased Income" by Doreen Bierbrier. There are some very detailed chapters on how to select tenants, and coupling these tips with ours should help you greatly.

Also, check out the agoodtenant.com Web site. This site has some great tenant screening tips that you can read and digest. Plus, the site is designed to help you fully screen prospective tenants, and even rank them for you. There are some costs involved, but this Web site is a wonderful tool to help you find the best tenants.

Chapter 5

The Ground Rules

The ground rules chapter will discuss the lease with option to buy, and the basic rules that we agreed upon at the onset of any arrangement. The lease that we used can be found in Appendix 2.

Try as we might, this is a dry topic, and thus, a particularly dry section. Sorry, we'll try to keep it light and interesting.

As part of the ground rules, we will also give some tips on things to do, and not to do with respect to setting precedents.

The lease that we used was cobbled together over the years from various example leases we had come across from various sources. The sources included books, other landlord's leases and some Internet information. While it is fairly complete, it has never been reviewed by a team of lawyers to determine if this can be considered a legal document that can stand the scrutiny of the bar association. Rather, we felt it was complete enough to form a binding contract between the tenant and landlord. We also hoped that it could provide a guide to the court should we get into a dispute that required legal intervention.

If you've read through it, you've probably noticed that it is a relatively complicated document. Much of the document is self explanatory, however. This Chapter will focus on the parts that may need further explanation.

Note, however, that this is a "Residential Lease With Option to Purchase Agreement". If you want to use this template as a Lease Only agreement, there are several sections that would have to be removed and several others requiring changes.

Lease Only

This section describes the general information on the lease form, and applies to both the "Lease Only" and "Lease With Option to Buy" situations. In addition, instructions for use as a "lease only" document are given.

For "Lease Only", Sections 7 and 19-23 should be removed, and the words lessee/buyer should be changed to just lessee. These sections will be discussed later when we talk about "Lease With Option to Buy".

In Section 2, the term can be whatever you want it to be. Generally, we used one year leases, and would renew the lease within 30 days of expiration of the previous lease. This gave us an opportunity to discuss the house and the tenant's general well being at least once a year. We also used this opportunity to talk about the lease option plan, and the progress being made to purchase the home.

You can use this same form for month by month lease agreements, as well.

Be sure to put the rent value into Section 3, and make it very clear if there is a prorated amount due because the person moved in on a date that was not the 1st of the month.

Section 4 deals with rent increases. We talk in more detail about rent increases in Chapter 7 – Taxes and Insurance. For good tenants we wanted to retain, we did not raise rent yearly, but only when property taxes increased (due to new levies). Thus, we were only passing along the property tax increases to the tenants.

You may decide to increase rent on a yearly basis. It all depends on your philosophy, your market and the neighborhood. If you can increase rent, by all means do so. Our market is not dynamic, but rather experiences slow, steady growth.

Section 5 is the Late Charge section. Be lenient at your own peril. However, there are maximum amounts allowable by law, so study your state/local ordinances to determine the maximum charges.

The Ground Rules

For many of our tenants, we let the first late payment (or two) go without charging any late fees. Guess what happened? The rent got later and later and later into the month. We started charging late fees, and we found that the rent was late less often. Notice, it still didn't mean the rent was on time all the time, but the tenants tried much harder to get you the rent money.

Generally, we allowed our tenants to pay their rent by the 5th of the month. The late charge was $25 with a daily fee of $10 beyond the 5th day of the month.

Now, to be fair, even when we charged the late fees, we didn't strictly adhere to the $10 per day. Let's say the tenants were 10 days late, and the rent made it to us on the 15th of the month. We should've charged them $125 extra. Instead, we'd probably tell them to pay an extra $40-50.

In hindsight, I think we would not bend on this policy. Our suggestion would be to write your late charges section in such a way that you will be comfortable enforcing it at all times. Then enforce it. My guess is you will have less late rent problems than we did.

We fell into the school of "give and inch, and they'll take a mile".

Section 6 discusses returned checks. We always charged $25 for this. Why? Several reasons. 1) Because it is an embarrassment to have to go to the bank and get this ugly "bounced check" message, complete with patented bank teller "dirty stare", 2) it is a waste of our time to have to go to the bank, then turn around and contact the tenant, and finally meet to get the proper payment and 3) the bank charges us about $15.

Mostly, we just got generally pissed off when a tenant stuck us with a bad check. Tell the truth, tell us you'll be late, but don't send us off to the bank to get "fined" and look like fools. We'll make you pay for this one every time.

After a couple of bounced checks, we would personally collect the rent in cash.

A Fool's Guide to Landlording

Section 8 lays out the requirements for terminating the lease. You must be clear with your tenants that a verbal notification is not sufficient. They must provide a written termination notice at least 30 days prior to the termination date.

Typically, we are talking about the "end of lease" date. If the tenant fails to provide the notice, and intends to stay in the house, then the lease reverts to a "month by month" status.

Occupancy rules are discussed in Section 9, and these rules are very, very important. The tenant must list out how many people intend to live in the home. During your selection process, you have already determined that the candidates you have selected will "fit" nicely into the home. Make sure that they haven't added more people to "their family" when they move in.

Also, if you are going to allow pets, have the tenant specifically list how many pets will live in the home, and have them give the pets names.

We found that people loved to tell us the name of their pets, and would be more than happy to list them. People seemed more responsible for their animals when their animal's names appeared on the lease. Don't ask why, because we haven't a clue.

The use (or non-use) of the property is listed in Section 10. Mostly, this section states what the property cannot be used for, such as (a) any activity which is noisy or dangerous, (b) repair of any vehicle, (c) any business, etc. Feel free to add anything we missed. The neighborhood may have zoning requirements as well.

Section 11 lays out the specifics the tenants obligations to pay all utilities. The gas and power are in the tenant's name, and are paid directly by the tenant. We paid the water and sewer bills, and were reimbursed by our tenants in the next rent payment.

Water and sewer are not generally turned off when the bills are not paid, so this was a precautionary measure by us to ensure that tenants never stuck us with months of unpaid water and sewer bills.

The Ground Rules

Be aware that the municipal water and sewer utilities can put a lien on your property, so ensure that the bills are paid on time and in full.

Section 12 talks about the insurance that the landlord provides for the home itself. Be sure to point out to the tenant that you are only providing insurance for replacement of the structure (due to fire, etc.) and not for the contents of the home. They must get their own renter's insurance.

It is important to lay out how many vehicles you will allow. Section 13 is the place to do this. Normally, we would allow one vehicle for each person of driving age. If you do not lay this out, you may find that your tenant's yard will look like a used car lot. I can't explain how this happens, but it does. So protect yourself.

In Section 14, the access rules are described. In the lease, we give the landlord rights to enter the property at reasonable times, WITHOUT NOTICE, to (a) inspect the property, (b) make repairs, (c) show the property, (d) leave written notices or (e) seize property after a default.

In fairness, we never entered the property (or even made a visit) without first calling. Even if our tenant was not going to be home, they would be contacted prior to our visit and would be allowed to basically approve the visit itself. We considered this a respectful way to handle visits.

However, if you have tenants that are damaging the property, or do not answer phone calls, then all bets are off. These folks you may have to "surprise" to get resolution.

Section 15 lays out the move-in condition, and basically serves as notice that the tenant accepts the condition of the house, AS-IS.

Section 16 is far more interesting, as it describes the responsibilities of the tenant and landlord, with respect to repairs. First, it lays out some general responsibilities. You may laugh at some of these, but you'd be surprised how often you might have to remind tenants that they have these responsibilities.

A Fool's Guide to Landlording

Some of the general responsibilities of the tenant include: (a) costs of plumbing stoppages caused by foreign or improper objects being flushed, (b) damages to doors, screens and windows, (c) damages resulting from leaving doors or windows open, (d) supplying and changing HVAC filters (good luck), (e) supplying and changing lights bulbs and smoke detector batteries, (f) replacement of yard and/or shrubbery caused by tenant damage, (g) prompt removal of trash (an area that you may need reminders), (h) cost of pest control, (i) lost or misplace keys and/or garage door openers, (k) lawn mowing and lawn maintenance and (l) driveway/sidewalk snow removal (if applicable).

Sounds basic, right. Well, you'd be surprised how many times you will have to refer the tenant back to this section to make them understand their basic responsibilities.

The second part of Section 16 describes the details of the repairs themselves. Basically, it says that the landlord is not obligated to repair something caused by the tenant, unless the condition was caused by normal wear and tear.

The ground rules are pretty basic, and indicate that you may need to turn off some utilities to make a repair, or you may have to wait until the next business day to get something repaired, unless it is an emergency.

Where this lease deviates, a bit, is in who should pay for the repairs. Because it was a lease/option agreement, we truly believe that this is the tenant's future home. Therefore, we thought that the little stuff should be repaired and paid for by the tenant. That is why we have a paragraph that allows you to set a value below which the tenant is responsible for repairs. We generally set the value to $200, but were never firm on this.

Many of our tenants made the small repairs without incident. Some of these were "nice-to-haves", like putting in new faucets (because they wanted something more stylish), or changing the handles on the cabinets.

In some cases, the tenants were making a repair or change that was less than $200, but we helped pay for because they were such good tenants. One example involved a tub surround that was around $150, but we paid half. The tenant put it in himself, and had already put several hundred dollars into the bathroom. This was the only time he asked us for financial support, and we gave it.

Remember, though, if they are actually going to buy the house, then they should be responsible for doing these things. Otherwise, they're getting their house fixed up at your expense.

The rest of the section discussed other areas such as prohibited acts, smoke detectors, yard maintenance and pool/spa maintenance.

Feel free to add onto this section, as required.

Section 17 lays out the tenant's remedies if the landlord fails to repair or remedy a condition. This is not a situation you want to get into, so be sure to work with your tenant to get the repairs done promptly, and to everyone's satisfaction.

Section 18 is the section where the tenant is encouraged to get homeowner's insurance for their belongings. To clarify this point, we always had the tenant put their initials at the bottom of this paragraph. We didn't want any trouble with lawsuits should the tenant burn down the house, and then sue us for the value of their belongings. Plus, we wanted to be sure the tenant's knew that they needed insurance to protect themselves and their belongings.

Section 24 talks about tenant default and acceleration of rent payments. For example, if the tenant is more than 3 days late for rent payment more than 3 months during a lease, then this signifies a breach of contract. The landlord could terminate a lease on these grounds alone. Of course, this is an option to the landlord. You may not choose to terminate at this point.

There are several other conditions listed in this section for breach of contract. You may take some of these out, or add your own.

The remainder of the Sections (25-36) involve various bits of legalize that you may want to keep or remove. Some of the sections may seem obvious, others may seem nebulous. For us, they seemed to cover the gamut of legal issues that we felt would potentially trip us up.

Lease With Option to Buy Sections

The "Lease With Option to Buy" sections are detailed below.

If you are intending to go with the "Option to Purchase", then Section 7 is very important to you. In the first paragraph of this section, you need to identify the value of the property. This is critical, so don't leave this blank. If you are signing a legal agreement giving someone first option to purchase the home, then you are giving this person a great power. With a word, he can exercise the option, and you will have to begin proceedings to sell the home to him within a very short, specified time period.

If you don't have a value in the right spot, Lord knows what he will try to negotiate as a price. Leave no stone unturned here. Find out the market value of the house, and base your price upon this. Our suggestion would be to update this amount yearly, just like the rent.

The second paragraph concerns the option money. In our case, we included the security deposit as option money. We would then combine that with whatever monthly stipend was set aside for the option money. Generally, the amount set aside each month was $50. So, this would amount to $600 per year being added to the option money account.

As you go into the next year's lease, be sure to update the blanks to reflect the fact that the option kitty is growing.

Section 19 talks about Encumbrances, which are permits or liens against the property. In this section, both parties are agreeing that neither will cause for a permit or lien to be attached to the property.

The Ground Rules

It is likely that you have a mortgage for the home, and this is considered a lien. However, the loan is for less than the property value, so this encumbrance is known and expected. The concern here is that you (or the tenant) might have some hidden encumbrance that would jeopardize the sale of the property.

Section 20 describes how the tenant should exercise the option. All that is required is a written notice from the tenant to the landlord requesting the option to be exercised.

The title obligations for the landlord are spelled out in Section 21. The landlord has 10 days (from the date the option was exercised) to execute and deliver all documents required to transfer the title to the property, along with any escrow instructions.

The landlord must ensure that the property is insurable, and free and clear of all liens and encumbrances except; (a) general and special taxes for the fiscal year in which the escrow closes and (b) exceptions, as agreed by the tenant, to be contained in the title report and all current easements, covenants and restrictions of record.

Section 22 details the escrow procedure, and the obligations of both the tenant and landlord. The landlord must: (a) deliver an executed general warranty deed to the property in recordable form conveying the title in the property to the tenant, and (b) the tenant should be credited with the "option money" that the landlord has been holding in escrow during the tenant's stay in the home.

Section 23 covers the prorations, closing costs, assumption and refinancing costs. It is important to break down the costs you will each be responsible for.

The landlord is responsible for the real estate transfer tax, title exam, title guarantee premium, prorations due the tenant, and one half of the escrow fee.

The tenant shall pay one half of the escrow fee, all of the assumption fees imposed by the secured lien holders, all loan discount points,

A Fool's Guide to Landlording

loan origination fees, appraisal fees, and all recording fees for the deed and any mortgage.

While this seems like a lot to know, you are just setting the framework for a business deal. If you tenant exercises the option to buy, you get plenty of help from the bank and the title company. Let them do the work. This document just helps spell out who will pay what and when.

Good luck, I hope you sell a house or two.

Chapter 6

Eviction

If you make it to the eviction phase, well then, congratulations. You are now enjoying the COMPLETE rental experience.

Never in my life did I think I would ever evict someone from our houses. We were just nice folks, and naively thought everyone acted the same way we did, more or less. I mean, come one, we could logically work our way through any situation. It was unfathomable to us that we would be involved with people for whom reason did not apply.

Hey, I told you were naïve, so back off!!

Well, people can, and do, change. And, other people can change you. In this case, we are a changed people, and in many ways, not for the better. I, for one, didn't really want to become more callous and bitter towards humankind as I got older, but I did as a result of the rentals. Being forced to evict two tenants was the epiphany that drove the change in our personalities and view of the world.

So, enough about psychology. Let's talk about something cheerful, like eviction.

There is a lot of good information published both in book form and on the Internet regarding eviction. We suggest you familiarize yourself with this information, and only use this chapter as a guideline. We have simply outlined the process, and this outline should apply everywhere in the country. However, there are some minor differences from state to state, and city to city, and you will need to review these to ensure that you conduct yourself properly.

First, it is important to point out that you must follow the rules perfectly when performing an eviction. If you make any mistakes at all, the judge will throw out the case, and you will have to start

A Fool's Guide to Landlording

the process all over again. During our two times in the courtroom, I would estimate that 25% of the cases were thrown out due to a technicality related to a minor mistake in following the process by a landlord, even cases where it was obvious that the tenant was clearly delinquent. The court is unforgiving towards landlords.

In fact, get used to the fact that the system is set up to protect tenants. A few crappy landlords have resulted in laws created that provide substantial legal barriers to eviction. So, you need to follow the rules and procedures. PERFECTLY!

If you don't believe us, go on the Internet, search for "eviction" and take a look at all of the web sites that pop up. Read some of the articles, and you'll quickly learn that most of this information is intended to screw you and allow your tenant to abuse the system as long as possible.

No one will take your side on this. Be a model landlord, follow the rules and the judge will likely rule in your favor. This is all you can hope for.

Reasons for Eviction

There are several reasons that may lead you to evict a tenant. However, for us, there was only ever one reason. Failure to pay rent money.

The two times we evicted tenants, it was because they wouldn't (or couldn't) pay their rent. By the time we officially pursued the eviction, we were already owed several months of back rent. We used eviction as a last resort. When we got to this point, we were cutting our losses, and there was no turning back. Had your chance(s), you blew it!!!

Now, with this experience, our recommendation to you would be to take a different approach. As soon as the rent is late, then enforce the late charges in the rental agreement (no exceptions). If the rent is still not paid a few days later, start the eviction process. Sounds cold, but you will either quickly get rid of a problem tenant, or send a message to your tenants that you are serious and not to be trifled with. Either way, these are good things.

The other reasons for eviction include: (a) serious damage to the property, (b) gang or drug related activity, (c) running an illegal business from the home and (d) simply refusing to leave at the end of a lease. Of course, this is not a complete list.

Another situation pertains to the scenario where you have a month by month lease. In The Liars horror story (Chapter 9), we talk about how we put these folks on a month by month lease so that we could use eviction as leverage to get them to pay their rent on time. This is the power of a month by month lease.

You give 20 days notice when you want to terminate the lease, and if they don't move out, you must use the eviction process to get them out.

Here is an example of how the eviction process works in our area. Be sure to check your local ordinances. You may find some differences in timing and procedure for your area.

Step 1 – The Eviction Notice

Before you can officially start the eviction process, you must inform your tenant that they have one last chance to pay (or fix the transgressions) before you can evict. This is not a verbal warning, this is a written warning.

In our area, the tenant has three days to pay after receiving a written warning.

Let's use non-payment of rent as the reason for our example.

You must provide a written notice to your tenant informing them that the rent is due within three days, or they must move out. How you deliver the notice is important. Remember, you must follow the procedure perfectly. One slip up, and the judge throws your case out.

A Fool's Guide to Landlording

So, here's what is required. First, try to deliver the notice in person to your tenant. If they are not available, then you are allowed to post it in a conspicuous place (a door works well).

If your tenant is home, and receives the notice in person, then you are not required to mail a copy. If the tenant is not home, and you have posted the note, then be sure to send a copy of the notice by registered mail.

If three days pass without resolution of the issue, then proceed to step 2.

You should be aware that some tenants will already know this game better than you. They know that, at this point, they could do nothing at all, and still remain in the house for about another 30 business days. Amazing, isn't it.

Our tenants, in both cases, played along with this step because they knew they could stretch it out even longer if they went through the process with us.

Step 2 – The Unlawful Detainer Action

Once the eviction notice from Step 1 expires (or the lease expires), you can begin the official process of eviction. This process is relatively easy, and requires you to file some forms at your local courthouse.

Some people hire a lawyer to handle the paperwork, and to show up in court to argue the case, but we did not do this. A lawyer significantly increases the cost of eviction, and if you are a reasonably competent individual, you can handle the duties of eviction.

However, if you don't want to take the time away from work, or, you really don't want to enter into this conflict, then there are plenty of law firms that handle evictions. Be sure to ask prospective lawyers how many evictions they do a year. If you're going to pay for it, then get someone who does this for a living. You can be sure they'll get the tenant out as quickly as possible.

Eviction

Anyway, if you're doing it yourself, get on down to the local courthouse and fill out the required paperwork. Costs vary by state and city, but the whole eviction process should only cost a few hundred dollars, at maximum. Get on the Internet, or call the local courthouse and find out the fees that will be required to file the paperwork. You will need the greenbacks to pay to file the forms. Credit cards won't cut it. Remember, this is the government, and convenience and service are words not in their vocabulary.

Once you have filled out the paperwork and filed the documents, the process has begun. A Summons and Complaint have been registered with the court.

The Summons and Complaint is a legal document that your tenants cannot ignore. They must respond. The document is "served" either by a sheriff, a bailiff or a private company. In most cases, cities contract with private companies to "serve" summons documents to citizens.

The landlord cannot "serve" the document. The court wants to be satisfied that the tenant has been given adequate opportunity to be appraised of the situation, and this is best left in the hands of professionals. So, file your paperwork and let the system take care of the details.

Step 3 – Wait, wait, wait!

Step 3 is not really a step at all for the landlord. It's more of a time period.

The tenant is required to respond, in writing, to the summons by the deadline stated in the summons. Normally, the tenant will have 5 days to respond.

You have to put this in perspective. The Unlawful Detainer document is a "Complaint", and you are effectively accusing your tenant of malfeasance of some form or fashion. This requires the tenant to provide a response to the court, simply called the "Answer".

The "Answer" is your tenant's side of the story. It must directly respond to your "Complaint". Expect your tenant to deny all of your allegations, and provide their own allegations of your misconduct, whether there was any or not. The lies that will be told here boggle the mind. Lying to a court seems to be an art for some people.

So, the "Answer" will be on its way back to the court within 5 days, and the next step in the process will begin. But, take note, there are a number of other things your tenant can do in the meantime, and especially if they obtain legal advice.

There are all sorts of ways to delay the process, and lots of different angles, and paperwork that can be taken and filed. If you are in the middle of this process, take some time and do some research on the Internet to see what is possible. Hopefully, this won't happen to you.

And, here is the biggest tip you will ever get. DO NOT take any money from your tenant once this process begins. If you accept any amount of money at all, this will be brought up at the trial, and will be viewed very negatively by the judge. Our judge threw out every case where the landlord accepted money, even if it was a token amount.

Resist the temptation to take the money. They will offer it, believe me. You will be tempted because you know this is the last money you will ever see from these people, but just DON'T DO IT!!!

Step 4 – The Trial

After the "Answer" is filed, the court will set a trial date. In our community, these are not trials by jury, but rather are presided over by a judge only. There are other procedures in other parts of the country, and you should familiarize yourself with your local laws.

In our case, we simply had to meet with a judge who handles housing issues.

Expect the trial date to be set 2-3 weeks after the court receives the "Answer".

Not that I'm counting, mind you, but let's do the math to this point. 3 days to serve notice, a day to file for eviction, another 2 days for the tenant to get the "Complaint and Summons", 5 days to respond with the "Answer", and 3 weeks until a trial date.

So, by the time you get to trial, you have already waited 28 working days. This is nearly 6 weeks. It's true, get used to it.

If you decide to handle the trial yourself, which we did, here is what happens, at least in our neck of the woods.

First, plan on taking the whole day off of work for the trial date. In our case, the housing cases were usually handled in a morning session. The way it works here, all of the housing cases are compiled, and once a week or so, the judge presides over all of the cases in a 3 hour session.

When you get to the courthouse, you locate the courtroom and find the posted case list. All of the cases that will be handled by the court will be listed in the order of appearance. I don't know who controls the order, but there doesn't seem to be any rhyme or reason to it.

Hope that your case is listed early on the docket. Otherwise you will have to sit through all of the other cases waiting for yours.

Evicting The Liars

The first time we did this, our case was one of the last to be handled. For us, this was sort of a blessing in disguise, because we had never been through this, and we were able to learn how to behave real time by watching. This was very important, as the ratio was about 3 to 1. For every one person that handled themselves professionally and appropriately, there were three people who taught us what NOT to do.

Most of the tenants that showed up were very emotional and unstable in the courtroom. But, so were a lot of the landlords.

We were surprised to learn that there were several people who were frequent participants in this court. One guy was a manager of an apartment complex that apparently had a lot of evictions, and he and the judge were quite friendly. He was great to watch, and we learned how to present our case from him. Succinct, to the point, the problem was laid out, and his expectations were clear. The boy didn't lose a case.

Finally, it got to be our turn, and we stepped up to the bench. We were surprised, but our tenants decided not to show. This was a relief, as we were dealing with The Liars here, and I expected a "he said, she said" moment in front of the judge, which I knew by watching her, that she wouldn't like it. The Liars would've muddied the situation beyond repair.

But, by being a no-show, we presented our case, answered two questions, and "bang went the gavel", we got the judgment we were looking for.

Because The Liars had children, the judge gave them the maximum amount of time to vacate. This was 10 days in our case. Some localities may have different rules or time periods. Anyway, they were informed by the court that they had so many days to vacate.

Evicting The Druggies

Our second time through the system, our luck had somewhat improved. We were the third case on the docket. However, Mr. Druggie had decided to attend. He begged me to reconsider while we were waiting for the courtroom to seat us.

As I've said in Horror Stories, I liked this guy personally, but it is too late to beg forgiveness now. I told him he had multiple chances, and he forced us to take this route, which we did not enjoy. Tough luck, fella.

We got called up to the bench, and Mr. Druggie was shaking with nerves. We presented our case, and I am still surprised to this day what happened next. The judge asked Mr. Druggie if the various charges were true, and lo and behold, he said "Yes, Ma'am, it's true". He told the truth. He really was an honest fellow.

He tried to explain why he was having trouble, but the judge cut him off rudely. She'd been through this too many times. She was all business.

She asked him one more question. "Do you have children?". He answered no, and she told him he had 7 days to vacate. "Bang went the gavel."

Step 5 – Wait, wait, wait

Yep, back to waiting. Now, you're probably thinking that you can drive on over to the house on the prescribed day and march on into the house and take back control. Well, not quite.

You see, while the tenants have been told to move out in a specified number of days, they know that there will not be a sheriff present to throw them out on that particular day. So, you can count on the fact that your tenants will find out how to play the system.

You don't have to be Einstein to contact your local courthouse and find out when the Sheriff does housing evictions. In our city, the Sheriff did the East Side of the city during the first week of the month and the West Side during the third week of the month. Our houses were on the West Side, so the Sheriff wouldn't be out until the third week of the month.

In the case of The Liars, they were supposed to vacate sometime during the first week of a particular month. They didn't. They stayed until the third week and milked it for all it was worth. They even found out the day the Sheriff was due to arrive, and finally left the night before. Nice people, eh?

The Druggies were a little better. They were out on the day they were supposed to go, even though they could've also milked it for another two weeks. Honestly, I don't think they even bothered to check with the Sheriff's schedule, they just got out when they were told to.

Total Time Elapsed

So, let's finish our math problem. At last count, we were up to 28 working days to get to the trial date (6 weeks real time).

Worst case, then, let's say your tenant gets 14 days to vacate (that's real days, not working days). Then, the sheriff takes another two weeks to get to your neighborhood.

Now, the 6 weeks turns quickly to 10 weeks. This was roughly how long it took in both cases for us. 10 weeks; 2.5 months.

And don't forget the best part. The reason we evicted them was for not paying rent. By the time we decided to evict, our tenants were about 3 months behind. Since you cannot take any money from your tenants during the eviction process, they just lived rent free for almost another 3 months.

So, the grand total is 6 months of lost rent. Plus, you have to fix the house up again and re-rent it, which could take at least two months. So, these wonderful people just cost you at least 8 months of rent.

Hope you enjoyed making that extra mortgage payment for 8 months.

Beware the Bankruptcy

Thankfully the laws have changed a bit in this area due to the deluge of bankruptcy filings over the past couple of years. But, in our day, the laws had yet to change.

It used to be that a tenant could file bankruptcy to stop an eviction. Now, this didn't happen to us exactly this way, but rather, our tenant (The Liars) filed for bankruptcy two months after moving into our home. This is when they stopped paying rent, the first time. We eventually got this straightened out, and made it a few more years with these guys, but we learned some things about eviction even in the early days.

Eviction

What we learned was that there are extra steps to go through when someone files for bankruptcy while you are trying to evict them. If they file for bankruptcy after the trial date, then the bankruptcy cannot delay the move out date.

However, if they file for bankruptcy anytime before the trial, then the process is a bit more complicated. In our day, the filing could've delayed the eviction process indefinitely. It was up to the bankruptcy judge, and frankly, the landlord is down pretty low on his list of priorities.

These days, things move a bit quicker. Still, if the bankruptcy is filed before the trial, you will need to go to the Bankruptcy Court and get permission from the judge to continue with the eviction. Once you get his permission, you must go back to the Housing Court and ask them to set a new date for the trial.

We all know how fast the wheels of government turn, so you can count on this process adding yet another month to your 3-6 month eviction ordeal. It could be worse though. If the laws hadn't been changed, you could be waiting forever.

Chapter 7

Taxes and Insurance

As they say, there are only two sure things in life, Death and Taxes. There's not much one can do about the first bit, but one can certainly have some influence on taxes. The main reason we got into the rental business was as an investment vehicle with serious tax advantages. So, this whole game is about taxes. Now, there are two areas of taxes we cover here. The first is property taxes, and the second is income taxes.

Property Taxes

Property taxes are the taxes you pay to your local government that are a function of the value of the home. These taxes are split many ways, with some money going to local government, and in Ohio anyway, the lion's share going to the school district.

The taxes are tied to the property value, and remain fixed from year to year, unless new levies are passed by the way of an electoral vote. Also, property taxes can change (read, go up) whenever the home is reappraised by the county. This occurs every three years in our area, and when the home is purchased.

When you set your rent, be sure to include enough margin so that you can cover the mortgage and the property tax. (You will also need to add a bit for insurance on the home, but this is a usually a minor amount, and depends on where the house is located. In Cleveland, this amounts to about $20 a month.)

Most of the time, we only raised the rent if the property taxes were increased substantially. This normally happens every three to four years, and is generally the result of a new school levy being passed. We never raised rents yearly. Only when we had to due to property tax increases.

In your market, you may want to raise the rent on a yearly basis. See what everyone else in your marketplace is doing, and do the same. Just don't price yourself out of the market, or your competition will eat your lunch.

Also, give a break to good tenants. Don't give them any reasons to move on. You want to keep these folks.

Income Taxes

If you are like us, you are investing in property in the hopes that you can achieve a reasonable rate of return on the property when you eventually sell it. Also, you are hoping to generate a little cash flow for which the taxes are deferred until you sell the property. If done correctly, you can achieve both of these goals quite nicely.

If you've never had rental property, then learning the ropes of tax law in this area is a daunting task. When we started, most people either did their own taxes by hand, or used a tax preparation service, like HR Block. Computer programs were not yet available to the masses, and everything was done by hand. Today, computer programs, such as TurboTax®, (a registered trademark of Intuit Corporation), have simplified this job substantially.

By all means, if you are not currently using a tax program and you are hell bent on having rental property, then invest the time and money to learn how to use a program. We use TurboTax®, and it has been a Godsend.

Before the age of computer tax programs, we had to learn which forms would be required to do taxes for rental property, then request all of the forms and associated publications that related to this topic. There are many.

We had to study these horribly tedious forms and try to understand what they meant. The depreciation schedule (Form 4506) alone took me weeks to understand. Computer programs have made this much easier now.

Still, we recommend that you familiarize yourself with the details of tax law regarding rental properties. You should try to read the publications to give you insight into how you should handle the taxes in this area. Then, get yourself a program and learn how to use it.

If you are like us, you will be adding your rental property information to your normal tax form. This means you will need to become familiar with Schedule E.

The Schedule E Form

The Schedule E form is used for Supplemental Income and Loss, and is the main rental property tax form, much like Schedule A is the main form for itemized deductions. Get a copy of the Schedule E and follow along with this discussion. We have many tips and pointers that will make this process much easier for your first time through. But be forewarned, this is still a painful process.

Passive Investment My Butt

In the general instructions for the Schedule E, you will notice a discussion regarding whether you are "At-Risk" or "Passive" with regard to the rental property. In most investments, your ability to deduct your losses is limited if you are a "Passive" investor.

Simply put, a "Passive" investor is someone who does not "materially participate" in the rental activity. A limited partner falls into this category. The Schedule E instructions devote a page to describing passive activities.

Generally, if you own, maintain and handle the finances of the rental property, you can safely assume that you are an "At Risk" investor, and not a "Passive" investor. Even though you will likely be "At Risk", the government considers rental property a "Passive" investment. Obviously, the bureaucrats that wrote these rules were never landlords.

The reason that this is important is that "Passive" losses are limited to the extent of income from passive activities only, if you are married and "filing separately". That means that if have a loss on the property, you cannot deduct it as such on your taxes. You will have to put a $0 on the 1040 for your rental activities.

But, if you make money, believe me, you will have to claim this as income.

If you are single or married filing jointly, this does not apply. However, in all cases, there is a limit of $25,000 that you can claim as a loss from rental properties. Generally, this type of deduction would only occur if you have many rental properties, and had some large expenses, such as fix up of new properties.

If you have a single property, and achieved a loss of $25,000 or greater, well then, you had a very bad year. You might want to reconsider this "business".

Fortunately, there are exceptions for certain rental property activities. These are complicated, and again you should reference the tax instructions, but here is a summary.

To be considered an "At Risk" investment, you must meet all three of the following conditions.

1) Your only passive activities are your real estate activities
2) You have no unallowed passive losses from prior years
3) You meet the following criteria if you have a passive loss
   a. You actively participated in all of the rental property activities
   b. Your overall net loss was less than $25,000
   c. You have no unallowed credits from passive activities
   d. Your adjusted gross income (of course) is $100,000 or less

Complicated, you bet. Important. Definitely.

Tax preparation for rental properties is gruesome, but crucial. Audits are painful and time consuming, so be sure to read and re-read the Schedule E instructions.

Get Organized and Avoid IRS Audits

The first tip is to save every single receipt. If you try to manage this business without receipts, you will eventually be audited and you will have no substantial proof as to your expenses on the

Taxes and Insurance

rental property. The government is heartless in this situation, and will disallow anything for which a receipt is not available.

In fact, this is one area that the government tax auditors look to as a means of increasing their bonuses. If you didn't know, tax auditors get a percentage of any additional taxes they can prove that you should owe, versus what you paid. If you are without receipts, some tax auditors may have a field day with you, as they will look at this as an opportunity to increase their pay. I know, it's difficult to believe that your lovely government would do this to you, but believe it.

With a boxful of receipts, neatly organized, you will be amply equipped for any battle with the government, should one ensue. If you never get audited, God bless you. But if you do, you will thank us profusely for this advice.

We number all of our receipts and keep them in a secure place. Each house has it's own set of receipts. In addition, we enter all of the expenses on a line by line basis in an Excel® (a registered trademark of Microsoft) spreadsheet. This allows us to document the expenses, and to keep track of the cash flow from the house at any time during the year, be it negative or positive.

We can tell you at any point during the year whether the house is bleeding money like a stuck pig, or whether we are making ends meet. This is important information, and if done right, will reduce the amount of time filling out tax forms in April.

An example of our Excel® spreadsheet is included in Appendix 3. The columns are set up to ensure you have the data inputs you need for the Schedule E form. Of course, you'll want to contact an accounting professional to discuss financial aspects applicable to your situation.

Income – Line 3

The first column in our Excel® spreadsheet tabulates that amount of rent you have collected for the year (the revenue). Because our business model revolves around a lease with option to buy

A Fool's Guide to Landlording

lease, we actually handle the option money with the second column.

Since the option money is technically set aside into a savings account specifically for down payment money, it is not considered as income to the business. So, to make the data inputs, we put the option amount into column 2 and input the difference between the rent payment minus the option amount into column 1. The total of column 1 is then the total revenue generated by the business. This information is then transferred to Line 3, Column A of the Schedule E.

Taxes on the money that has been deferred do not have to be paid until the house is sold. If the tenant buys the house, then the option money will be recharacterized as income that adds to the basis of the house upon sale. The same is true, even if the house is sold to another buyer. Keep the option money in escrow until the home is sold.

The next section of the Schedule E is the Expenses section. Again, we keep track of all of these areas in a line by line fashion in our Excel® spreadsheet, so at the end of the year we can tally up the totals and enter them into the Schedule E.

It is important to remember one rule of expense accounting. Your time and labor are worthless to the government. So, any time you spent fixing up the property, or any capital investments or capital improvements are not to be deducted as expenses. Just wait and see how much pain this will cause you when you make your first small profit, and then have to pay the government tax money on your sweat equity. You'd think Uncle Sam was right there with you when you were putting in that new toilet, and slopping out the clogged drains.

Nope, get over it. Here are a partial listing of the expenses that you can include:

Advertising – Line 5

You will undoubtedly experience some advertising expenses in the first year that you rent out your property. These expenses are quite

Taxes and Insurance

obvious, and include such things as newspaper advertisements, lawn signs, flyers and any other expenses related to the search for potential tenants. These expenses should generally be quite small in the overall scheme of things.

In the following years, if your tenant signs on for additional years, you shouldn't have any expenses in this area at all.

Auto and Travel – Line 6

There are so many rules in this area, we would advise a read through of the details. However, if your life is not too complicated, chances are that you will be able to keep track of your miles during the year, and multiply these miles by 36 cents to get a value for this entry. (Get the current value, as this changes yearly.)

You will be surprised how many miles you will put on your vehicle(s) when you own rental property. We used to include our mileage on our Excel® spreadsheet, in detail, trip by trip. After we gained some experience, we found that the number of miles we traveled in rental related business was nearly the same year after year, so we didn't bother keeping detailed records in later years. This was mainly because all of our rental houses were in the same area, and thus, the same distance from our residence.

For us, the mileage was usually about 1500 miles per year, and was worth about a $500 deduction.

If you're new to the game, or if your houses are located in varying distances from your home, then we'd recommend you keep detailed records of your trips. By the way, it is never a bad idea to keep detailed records, regardless of the situation.

Cleaning and Maintenance – Line 7

This expense is quite self explanatory. The expenses in this category ought to include regular cleaning expenses, such as steam cleaning the carpeting, and regular maintenance, like sealing a deck or driveway.

A Fool's Guide to Landlording

Commissions – Line 8

Since there is no description of this item in the instructions, and we always managed our business ourselves, we believe that we probably (a) never had an expense in this area and (b) if we did, we're not sure if this was the right place to put it.

So, we're not sure why or how you would need to pay a commission to anyone, but if you did, we're pretty sure you'd enter it here.

Insurance – Line 9

The personal belongings of the tenant are the responsibility of the tenant. You do not need to seek insurance to cover the personal belongings of your tenant. This is similar to the "homeowner's insurance" that you likely have on your own personal belongings.

However, you should have insurance for the property itself. The value of this type of insurance should be set at a value that will ensure that you could rebuild the home on the same piece of ground in current dollars. This insurance is intended to prevent a major loss of capital, (your rental home).

We also recommend an umbrella insurance policy to protect you from the unforeseen. We live in the United States of America, and if you haven't noticed, we are producing more lawyers than teachers in this country. These folks need to earn a living, and too many of them are doing this on the backs of hard working folks. (That'd be you.) If someone trips over a crack in your sidewalk for example, you want to be covered in case they call an ambulance chaser and sue you for your entire net worth.

Also, be aware that you can reduce the premium by both shopping around and by providing safety devices such as fire extinguishers, smoke alarms and carbon monoxide detectors (watch this one, see the Horror Stories with respect to The Losers).

Taxes and Insurance

Legal and other Professional Fees – Line 10

The only acceptable fees in this area are the fees you pay to help you with your taxes. This would include fees for legal advice as well as fees related to the preparation of tax forms related to the real estate activity.

Management Fees – Line 11

If you own an apartment complex, or have so many rental properties that you turn to a real estate management company, you can deduct their fees in this entry. Remember, you can't deduct your time and effort, so don't think of charging $100 per hour for your time to manage the rental property.

Mortgage Interest – Line 12

This is a pretty straightforward entry. If you have a mortgage on the home, then enter the amount of interest that you paid for the year in question. You can deduct only the interest for the year in question, so don't play games and try to deduct "pre-paid" interest. Points and certain fees related to obtaining the loan must be amortized (deducted over the life of the loan), and should not be included here.

Figuring out what needs to be amortized can be a daunting task the first time through, so be sure to read Publication 535 to get the details or talk to your accountant.

Other Interest – Line 13

If you borrowed money from your uncle, or any other place that is not a financial institution, you could end up with broken knuckles or legs if you fail to meet their timelines. But, at least you will be able to deduct the interest in Line 13 of the form. This entry is set up for interest paid that does not show up on a 1098 form.

Repairs – Line 14

This is a tricky area in rental property ownership. The cost of repairs allowed in this section are limited to repairs that are

A Fool's Guide to Landlording

required to keep the house in good working order. Repairs that add value to the home or extend life to some part of the home are not allowed here.

Examples are the best remedy for understanding this. Fixing a broken pipe, painting a room, replacing a problem electrical outlet and things of this nature are considered qualified expenses for Line 14.

Replacing a roof, a driveway, siding, gutters, hot water tank, carpeting and similar projects are considered to either have added value to the home, or have extended the life of a component of the house, and are not deductible in this section.

The costs of these types of repairs are deductible, but they must be amortized, or deducted over the expected life of the repair, and will be considered later on, in the depreciation section.

Be careful in this area, and have extremely good records. Most landlords that we have known have been audited because they did not amortize a large repair expense, but rather, tried to write it off as one lump sum. This can trigger an audit alert from an astute IRS agent. And, these are easy picking for the IRS folks. They will win, and you will lose. Save yourself the hassle, and the fines.

Supplies – Line 15

This entry is fairly general, and can be used for all sorts of expenses related to your rental property. There is no detailed description on the instructions form, so we made some assumptions for how to use this entry.

Our advice would be to use this as the catch all for all of the things you bought for the rental property that are legal, but yet do not fit snugly into any of the other categories.

You, like us, will undoubtedly spend lots of time (and money) at places like Home Depot and Lowe's. You will have very long, itemized receipts from these stores where you bought all sorts of

Taxes and Insurance

things from soup to nuts. Many of the things that you bought are truly supplies, and should be entered here.

For example, things like light bulbs, towels, razor blades, wallpaper remover, carpet cutters, tools, etc. were tackled under this heading. Literally, the list goes on and on and on. Generally, our entry in Line 15 was the largest amount in any of the other expenses.

To get a rental property up and running, and keep it humming, you need to buy a bunch of things from hardware stores as the year goes by. It is just a fact of life.

Taxes – Line 16

Most cities/counties assess a property tax on homes. We used this entry simply to enter the amount of property tax we paid on the home for the year.

Some places may have additional taxes related to home ownership, and possibly rental ownership. These taxes should be included here as well.

Utilities – Line 17

As we mentioned in previous chapters, we never trusted tenants to pay the water and sewer bills. Our tenants were responsible for the electric and gas bills. Why? Because electric and gas companies are forgiving only to a point. If you don't pay, they will shut you off. This is generally incentive enough for tenants to pay these bills. Plus, the bills are in the tenants name, and do not transfer to the house if the tenants skip town.

However, the water and sewer bills are a different story. First, the city will almost never shut you off, no matter how overdue your bills. And, if the tenant skips town, the bill reverts to the property, not the tenant, and you get stuck with the bill.

So, we pay the water and sewer, then back charge the tenant on a quarterly basis. We need to deduct the cost of these utilities on

Line 17, because they have been added into the income amount shown in Line 3.

Other – Line 18

If you have expenses that are deductible, but do not fit into any of the above categories, then include then in Line 18. Be sure to list the expense, and explain what it is. If it doesn't fit anywhere else on the form, you can be sure the IRS wants some sort of explanation as to what the expense pertains to. Without some verbiage, you will likely be challenged for your expenses here.

Depreciation

Depreciation shows up in Line 20 of the form, as innocuous as could be. Well, thank God for TurboTax® you lucky son of a gun. Because you will be spared all of the pain that we had to go through when we first started doing this blasted form in 1993.

Tell you what, just for fun, print out a copy of Form 4562 and read through it one night for some light reading. Now, assuming you're not an accountant, read through this bogus document and tell me when you start getting bleary eyed. Come on, how far did you make it?

Page 3, well done!!!

My first time, I had to re-read this damn thing several times before I could even begin to figure out how to depreciate the home, and the several repairs we made to the thing prior to renting it. I mean, we had to figure out how to depreciate the carpet, the points, etc. What a daunting task.

You should read through this once just to give you and idea of what is going on, and to show you what the tax program is doing. But, I dare say, I wouldn't advise that you try to understand it. As an engineer, you should respect my opinion when I tell you that this was a very difficult homework assignment.

I will say this, however, once I figured it out, it was like a light bulb coming on. It just made sense one day, and I'll never forget how

Taxes and Insurance

things are depreciated forevermore. This has helped me at work when we get into financial discussions and decisions involving capital investment in our offices and plant. Good stuff.

Anyway, the advent of tax programs has made this so much better. Using the wizard, you will be guided through this section. Even if you don't know what is going on, you can choose the default settings and come out smelling like a rose.

Best yet, when you do the following year's taxes, you can import this information, and the programs are smart enough to take on the cumulative depreciation year by year.

So, even though we didn't get the benefit of this simplification the first year, we have enjoyed the benefits of having to only input the data once, and having the program manage the depreciation year by year.

It is so powerful, that you don't even have to worry about the depreciation amortization issues when you sell property. When you sell, you have to figure out how much has already been amortized, then write off the rest in a lump sum fashion. If you forget to do this, you will not be taking advantage of all of your expenses. These programs do this automatically for you. Cool.

The Results

Once you plug all of these numbers in, you will get a final tally as to whether you show a gain or a loss on your property. Typically, a gain is taxed at a 25% tax rate, irrespective of your income bracket. It is treated like a special sort of income, much like a capital gain, but with its own tax rate.

For 2003 anyway, if you have a loss, and it is below $25,000 (married filing jointly), then this amount will come off of your income on page 1 of the 1040 form. Any savings in taxes will depend on your income tax rate.

This is where the discussion in Chapter 2 comes into play with respect to how you bought the home. If you used the "no money down" approach, and you priced your rent at market value,

A Fool's Guide to Landlording

then you will likely show a very small positive cash flow before depreciation. After depreciation, you will show a substantial loss. This loss is a deferred loss (e.g. not real in the present year), and this allows you to reduce your taxable income. Thus, this approach allows you to get a tax benefit that is essentially allowing you to defer your tax liability until you sell the property.

You see, once you sell the property, you must then take into account the amount you depreciated. So, the depreciated value is subtracted from the house selling price, and you pay tax on the difference.

So, you're not getting away from your tax liability, you are just deferring it. The thought is that you will defer the tax liability to a time when you are perhaps retired, and earning less money and in a lower tax bracket, than at present.

If you bought the house with 20% down, it is likely that you will show a slightly higher cash flow than the above case. You may then either show a small gain or a small loss after depreciation, depending on your expenses in the home for the year.

If you took the third approach, and paid for the house outright, then you will show a substantial cash flow, and will show a substantial profit even after depreciation. You will pay a considerable chunk of taxes on this income, and you should plan for this during the year by paying quarterly taxes on this expected income so as not to run into penalty situations when you file your taxes.

Chapter 8

Internet Sites and Books for Landlords

When we started out in the rental business, Al Gore hadn't invented the Internet yet. Now that the Internet is here, you have so many more resources at your fingertips to help you with your rental business than ever before.

I must admit, however, that book publishing DID exist back when we started, and yet, we didn't read a single book before jumping into this business. This is not an unusual approach for a couple of engineers. We never read the "user's manual" until something breaks, or doesn't work right. Yep, we started reading the books when things began to go poorly.

This chapter will highlight several of the Internet sites and books that we found particularly useful.

Internet Sites

Can you imagine your life before the Internet? Most of us had a life (some of us longer than others) before the Internet, but it is hard to fathom how we got things done in these prehistoric times.

The Internet has simply made life easier by providing access to information. And, by virtue of the ease of dissemination, there is more information available than ever before.

This is true for the rental property business.

This is not intended to be a complete listing of all landlord Web sites. Rather, this is a list of several very good Web sites that can help you with your rental property issues. You will undoubtedly find other sites that will be useful to you, and when you do, we encourage you to "Go For It".

1. *A Good Tenant* (agoodtenant.com)

This Web site is chock full of great information, and helpful features. You can use the site to help you screen and select tenants, recover rent and evict tenants, amongst other things.

Get on this Web site and check out the "Free Screening Tips", first and foremost. We found this to be an outstanding feature of the site, because it offered step by step tips of what to do and what to look for during the tenant screening process.

Couple this information with our chapter on tenant screening, and the chapters of our recommended books below, and your chances of signing on a quality tenant is significantly increased.

The Web site also provides several resources for a fee. The main services of interest are:

Tenant Screening Reports

The Web site provides a link to a complete tenant screening service. The service has access to many detailed databases that it uses to screen the quality of your prospective tenant. The databases include:
    a) Credit report
    b) Public records (e.g. bankruptcies, law suits, etc.)
    c) Address history
    d) Evictions
    e) Driver's license verification
    f) Banking habits

Prices for this detailed screening report can be as low as $10 for a basic tenant screen, to as much as $30 for the deluxe screening service. The Deluxe service includes searching national databases and providing services, as outlined here:
    a) National consumer credit database
    b) Credit and collection accounts
    c) Statistical risk predictor for tenant
    d) Fraud detection
    e) Complete list of credit grantors and information to confirm accounts

Internet Sites and Books for Landlords

f) Multi-State eviction search
g) Possession and money judgments
h) Delinquent Tenant Cooperative search
i) Free Matchmaker
j) National criminal search
k) Social Security Number verification
l) Sex offender search
m) Terrorist database search
n) National address history
o) Public records and bankruptcy
p) Age and employment verification

All of this for only $30!!!!

We would recommend that you perform the deluxe screening for your top three candidates. This will likely help you to determine if your top three are as good as they seem. Plus, this significantly increases the likelihood that you will avoid tenant problems down the road due to financial problems, such as bankruptcy or insolvency.

Tenant Invoicing

The Web site also provides a link to a tenant invoicing service. This service is geared for multi-unit apartment buildings with at least 25 units.

The service invoices each of the units of the apartment building for $2.50 per unit per month. If you have less than 20 units, the fee is still $25 per month. If you have more than 25 units, the fee goes down slightly with volume.

If you are renting out single family homes, then this service is likely not very practical, unless you have quite a few homes. If you have one home, then the $25 fee may be a bit too much to justify on a monthly basis.

Rent Collection

You can use a link in the Web site to connect you to a rental collection agency. This agency will collect the rent for either a

A Fool's Guide to Landlording

flat fee, or on a contingency basis. Obviously, the flat fee is less expensive, but there is no guarantee of collection. If you use the contingency method, you will only pay if the rent is collected. There are risks and rewards for both of these methods. Let's hope you never need this service.

Evictions

A very handy feature of this Web site is a link to an evictions service. The service will search a nationwide database to give you a complete eviction history of the tenant in question. All for $10.

At a minimum, run an eviction search on your prospective tenant. We would disqualify anyone who has EVER been evicted. You are not looking to rehabilitate your tenant, you are looking for someone responsible.

Delinquent Tenant Cooperative

The Delinquent Tenant Cooperative is a private organization formed for the exchange of information between rental property owners. The more information posted by each owner, the more powerful the cooperative becomes.

This is a great tool that can be used to find the "professional cheats". You can report and review records for tenants who have previously rented from a cooperative member. This is like a sophisticated chat room/database on tenants.

The database includes information such as:
    a) Delinquent payment history
    b) Property damage
    c) Suspected criminal activity
    d) Etc

Eviction Attorney Search

The last link on the Web site helps you find an experienced eviction attorney for your local area. Hopefully, you will never need these services, but it's nice to know that this resource is available.

Internet Sites and Books for Landlords

2. **Landlord Tenant Background Check** (tenantbackgroundcheck.com)

This is a somewhat basic, no-frills website that is a bit light on information. However, it does provide a background check service for only $20, and free registration

We never used this service, and would be more inclined to go for the deluxe service provided on other web sites. But, hey, if you're pinching pennies, you may want to try this reasonably priced service. Plus, they promise a report in an hour, so it's fast!!!

3. **The LandLord Protection Agency** (thelpa.com)

This Web site is best utilized if you become a member, which costs $70. Members get to enjoy many services, including:
    a) Deadbeat database
    b) Downloadable forms
    c) Credit report
    d) Available property lists
    e) Questions and Answers
    f) Much more….

However, there are many free services available to you on this Web site, even if you are not a member. We'd suggest you try some of the free services, which will help you decide if it is worth becoming a member.

The Web site was founded by John Nuzzolese, and he is a "nice guy" like we were when we started. He learned many lessons the hard way, like we did, and so you will benefit greatly from his experiences, and from being part of this group.

4. **US Legal Forms** (uslegalforms.com/landlordtenant/General.htm)

This Web site covers a broad range of areas, but its primary purpose is to provide access to legal forms in the United States. For our specific purpose, we will concentrate on the legal forms pertinent to landlords and tenants. The website address above reflects this approach.

A Fool's Guide to Landlording

This Web site is a super place to start to access and download standard forms pertinent to the rental property ownership business. Forms such as Lease Applications, Lease Purchase Agreements and Lease Termination Notices are available on this Web site. In fact, just about any type of form required is available.

The down side of the site is that it costs money to purchase forms. However you are allowed to view the form before purchase, via a *.pdf file.

In general, form prices ranged from $10-12, which is a reasonable cost for many documents, but especially a good Lease Agreement document.

Check out the various forms for information, and purchase any forms that fit your requirements. In many cases, this will be easy than creating a new form from scratch.

5. **Landlord Portal** (landlordportal.com)

This is a great "one-stop shop" website for landlords. There are many features to choose from, with the best being $5 tenant screenings. You can also look up the Federal Housing Laws by State.

Included in the many options on the Web site are discussion forums and a load of useful forms for use in the rental property business.

6. **Landlord** (landlord.com)

This is an extensive landlord Web site with tenant screening functions and a wealth of other services. This is also useful as a "one-stop shop" for landlords.

You will find loads of free rental advice, question and answer sections and discussion forums. Also, there is an impressive appraisal service which can be used to determine the value of a property before you buy.

7. ***House Detective*** (housedetective.com)

This site has links to foreclosed properties from private and government lenders with search capabilities. Access to the foreclosure section is an additional fee. Also provides links to qualified home inspectors in your area as well as tips on home repair and things to look for when assessing a property. Barry Stone is a syndicated columnist and the site and information is easy to read and understand.

Books

Similar to the Web site discussion above, this listing of printed materials is not intended to be the COMPLETE GUIDE to LANDLORDING. Rather, the books listed below are the ones that we have read, and have some information (e.g. opinion) to share.

1. Landlording by Leigh Robinson

Far and away, this was the best, most complete landlord/tenant book we came across in our research. I wish I read this one before I got into the rental business.

While Leigh has a positive outlook and it becomes very clear how difficult this business is as you read through this book. Leigh gives tons of great tips and useful information throughout the book.

On several occasions, we had "deja-vu" moments while reading the book. In black and white would be the CLEAR reason why we got into trouble with a tenant, and it was enlightening to read what we had done wrong. In all fairness, however, most of our problems were caused by our kindness, and some of the advice given, while perfectly valid, would be difficult for people like us to follow completely.

But, that is not a criticism of the book, but rather of our human nature. For many people, this book will alert them to problem areas and help them strengthen their resolve to properly manage the property.

A Fool's Guide to Landlording

We liked most of the book, and again it is worth a read. However, we particularly liked the sections about "Getting Good Tenants", "Rents, Rents, Rents", "Keeping Good Tenants", "Dealing With Problem Tenants", "Participating in the Section 8 Housing Program", and "Sources and Resources".

"Getting Good Tenants" does a great job of outlining how to screen without discrimination, which is not something we covered in this book because it was covered so well in the Landlording (and other) books. Leigh describes 10 Steps to getting good tenants, and we thought that he had perfectly outlined the best approach. The steps include things such as preparing the home for occupancy, showing the home, conducting the screening process, selecting the tenant and signing the lease. We really like the thoroughness of the screening discussion. Leigh certainly goes much further than we ever did.

"Rents, Rents, Rents" goes into great depth on all things related to rent, such as setting the rent, raising the rent, collecting the rent, etc. We haven't seen this much detail with respect to the rent value issues in any other medium.

"Keeping Good Tenants" provided some of the best advice in the book. Just like in any business, it is much more expensive to get new business, than it is to keep the business you already have. The same is true of tenants. If you have a good one, by all means, do everything in your power to keep the tenant. Leigh offers some very good tips on how to do this.

"Dealing With Problem Tenants" is the flip side of the previous paragraph. Here, you can find some sound advice on alternatives to eviction, and some tips on how to "outwit" you tenants. No one chapter in any book is ever going to solve all of your tenant problems, but the advice in this chapter should help you solve some of them. Some tenants just need to be evicted. This is covered as well.

"Participating in the Section 8 Housing Program" is a great chapter, and I mention it because you absolutely should read it. We did not cover this for several reasons. One reason was that we never had Section 8 candidates, because we leased to own.

Section 8 candidates are not allowed to live in a rental property that is being leased to own, it has to be a straight lease. So, we had no experience in this area. We felt no need to learn it in great detail, because Leigh has already covered this topic expertly in his book.

"Sources and Resources" is a must read chapter. This section lists resources in the following areas designed to help you in the rental property business.
    a) Associations and organizations
    b) Books
    c) Catalogs
    d) Computer Software
    e) Websites

Leigh's lists are more complete than ours, and should be used if you plan to research the business further.

Overall, this is the best rental property book that we found. Read it over and over again.

2. Managing Your Rental House For Increased Income by Doreen Bierbrier

Doreen's book is very practical, and deals more with the big picture issues of rental home management. We found this to be a very quick read that touched on a broad range of topics, ranging from finding a house to record keeping.

We found the sections on house inspection and finding good tenants to be the most useful chapters of this book. The house inspection section pointed out what to look for, and how to determine cosmetic problems from more major issues. Reading this should give you a leg up on knowing what to look for.

And, you just can't read enough advice on finding good tenants. Each book has several unique tips that you can apply. Doreen has more than just a few good tips here.

By all means, take a few hours and read this book.

3. The Landlord's Handbook by Daniel Goodwin and Richard Rusdorf

This book provides a lot of general information regarding rental property, and is best used in combination with other, more detailed books and Web sites.

One of the best parts of the book includes a wealth of information on tenant income requirements. In this section, detailed tables are shown that allow the landlord to assess how much income the tenant must earn in order to comfortably pay the rent he is asking. The rent range is from $300 to $1655 per month. The tables show the weekly, monthly and yearly income required to meet the desired rent.

Also included in the book are examples of various forms including application, lease and rental agreement forms.

4. The Landlord's Troubleshooter by Robert Irwin

This is another very good general text that is a must read for prospective landlords. Again, because the book is somewhat general, we recommend that you read it in conjunction with other more detailed books and Web sites.

The thing we loved best about this book was the 10 Golden Rules For Landlord's. Maybe that's because we broke these rules so often. Not to spoil Robert's thunder but here are the Golden rules, with some personal comments from us:

a) There are no acceptable excuses for late rent
    a. I wish we had followed this golden rule. Our tenants had so many good excuses, I've forgotten them all. We were suckers on this one, so don't you be. Obey the rule.
b) Accept cash only
    a. We accepted checks, and were burned a few times. Still, checks seem to work OK. But, get cash if you can.
c) No tenant is better than a bad tenant
    a. You may not believe this, and you certainly won't believe it if you are desperately trying to find a tenant while your house has been vacant for two months. But, until

Internet Sites and Books for Landlords

you've had a truly bad tenant, you will never be able to appreciate the power of this statement. Here's hoping you never do.
d) Always be friendly to, but never a friend of your tenant
   a. Business is business.
e) Don't enforce your lifestyle or family rules on your tenant
   a. This is none of your business. You may not understand it, or agree with it, but as long as the rent is paid, and the house is maintained, you have to let this one go.
f) A tenant who doesn't pay and stays is worse than a tenant who doesn't pay and moves
   a. Amen. This is just a matter of cost. You're going to lose money in both instances, it's just a matter of how much. The tenant who stays will cost you much more, as he will be able to milk the system for several months while you go through the eviction process.
g) Clean rentals attract clean tenants
   a. Well, they attract dirty tenants too. But, the point is that a dirty house will ONLY attract dirty tenants. So, by all means, show a clean, livable house so as not to scare away the clean, good tenants.
h) The best way to avoid an eviction is to not rent to that person in the first place
   a. Easier said than done. But, with all of the tenant screening tools now available to you, the odds of landing a good tenant are much better than they used to be. If you are not using tenant screening services, you are asking for trouble. This is a gamble not worth taking.
i) Never buy property more than 1 hour away from home
   a. This is sound, practical advice. You just cannot maintain your property and your tenant effectively if you live this far away. The hassle factor will increase exponentially as you get further and further from home.
j) Get everything in writing
   a. In this day and age, I am astounded that people still trust verbal agreements. With all the lawyers out there looking for work, you best get all the details nailed down in a written, signed document.

So, that was our favorite part.

A Fool's Guide to Landlording

But, the book also has a great example of a rental agreement form, which is similar to the one we share with you in Appendix 2.

Another really good chapter covered health and safety issues, which we did not cover extensively in this book. In particular, the chapter discusses lead disclosures, asbestos, carbon monoxide and radon concerns. Also, recommendations on installation of smoke detectors and fire extinguishers are also covered.

Finally, the book contains a good database of sample forms.

5. The Landlord Kit by Jeffrey Taylor

This book contains an extensive database of sample forms. In fact, most of the "kit" involves various sample forms. This is the most extensive database of forms we found in written form, and may be better than some of the Internet sites because these forms can be used for free.

6. Living With Tenants by Doreen Bierbrier

This book focuses on sharing a house with a tenant, and was not applicable to our business model. If this is how you plan to get into the business, then this is a must read book.

Chapter 9

Horror Stories

1. The Liars

Beware. This story should send chills down your spine. Not quite in a "Pacific Heights" kind of way, but about as close as you can get without the fear of death involved. The wisdom to be remembered here is ancient: "Give an inch, and they will take a mile".

We had already bought and rented several single family homes at this time, and we were getting just a little bit cocky about our abilities. We thought we had the perfect system for buying houses, fixing them up and screening good candidates for tenants.

The first two strengths, we definitely had. The last one wasn't a strength, it was luck. And our luck held out right up until the day the Liars came to stay.

This home was a HUD house. The people who owned it before bought it with the help of the HUD program, then couldn't make their payments. They were foreclosed upon, and the house was put on to the market, as is.

The home was attractive because it was in a nice area, and was just several doors down from the very first house we bought and were still renting. The area is called West Park, and has nice houses that provide reasonable capital appreciation.

A word about HUD houses. When you buy a HUD house, you have to be very careful. Usually, the power and water are turned off, so you don't know if there are any major electrical or plumbing issues. But hey, we were experienced, right?

We checked out the house extensively, and were fairly confident that it was sound. It only required some minor cosmetic repairs. No major problems.

A Fool's Guide to Landlording

For the most part, we were right. No major problems surfaced except that the government, in its infinite wisdom, made off with the main breaker package for the fuse box. Of course, there no longer is a replacement part on the market. What seemed to be a $20 fix would be more painful.

In fact, the cost was $400 to get a modern electrical box installed. Seems like the government took the opportunity to get the house's electrical system updated. Of course, they did it with our money. Nice.

But, the power and water were on now, and all was well in the house. For the most part, the fix up went well. However, we violated our own rules by buying this house, which only had 2 bedrooms. You will notice a trend here in the horror stories. For us, 2 bedroom = horror story. Run away.

Anyway, we turned the house in record time, and had it on the market in two weeks. So far so good.

Because of the desirable location of the house and the reasonable rent, we had dozens of applicants. While some of these applicants were sure to be clunkers, I'm sure there were some other good people in there as well. But, alas, we chose The Liars.

The Liars were such nice people to meet and talk with. How could you not love a young couple with two lovely young children? They seemed to have it together, and were just looking for a break. We seemed to be a match made in heaven.

I still believe that the Liars are basically nice folks. The problem is that I don't think they have any sense of responsibility. Of course, they will likely pass these wonderful traits down to their little ones, and the cycle will start afresh.

Little did we know that they also had two new car payments (zero down), several credit cards maxed out, new furniture (on lease) and a new dog. Of course, none of these credit issues turned up in our regular credit check. Guess why??? They bought all of this stuff (except the kids, I think) after they signed the one year lease/option agreement with us. Pretty crafty, huh? Don't get any ideas.

One week after the lease was signed, they moved in. The last happy day of my life, is what I would call it. Of course, we naively assumed that all of the stuff they brought with them they owned. Nope. All bought on credit during the past few weeks.

Hey, one has to fill a house if one wants to live in it, eh?

One month passed without incident, and all seemed right with the world. We raised a glass to another successful "sale", and felt especially good because we really thought we were giving a young family a leg up on the world.

By the second month, something was starting to smell bad. The rent check didn't show up on time. Normally, this didn't concern us much, as we were pretty flexible with people, and if rent showed up a few days late, we never even mentioned it. With some people, this is OK. With the Liars, we were being tested. Give an inch…..

On the third month, the rent check again didn't show up on time. This time, a week went by before we took action. Phone calls went unanswered. No one answered the door when we visited (although on several occasions it was clear someone was there). Three weeks went by, and still no contact and no rent check.

Since we had another home down the street, we were in the neighborhood quite often. We had some work to do at the other rental property on the same street, and figured we could keep an eye on the house for movement, and ATTACK.

On a bright and sunny afternoon, we stopped working when we saw them pull into the driveway with one of their shiny new cars. We walked over to them as they got out of their car, and my, the look on their faces would've stopped a clock. Busted!!!

They begged forgiveness and pleaded that they would straighten out this mess. There was trouble at her work, and she would be paid next week. Then we would get paid. Some horse crap story like this, anyway.

Wanna know how they straightened out the mess? Get ready, this is a doozy. They filed for bankruptcy.

For those of you unfamiliar with bankruptcy (God bless you), trust me, it is a mess. And, no one has a more difficult time than those of us who are owed by bankruptcy filers. That was their idea of cleaning up the mess. By moving the responsibility to everyone else.

Now, don't miss the irony here. The Liars knew full well that they were going to declare bankruptcy weeks (maybe months) earlier. So, what did these responsible individuals do? Well, they got themselves a house (with a year lease), and bought every possible thing they could think of with other people's money. They decided to make their problem everyone else's problem.

If you ever find yourself in this situation, you will understand immediately the feeling of hopelessness. When someone files for bankruptcy, they are protected from their creditors while the court figures out how to rectify the mess. You cannot evict someone in this situation. You cannot demand that they pay their rent. Nope. Instead, you must contact the bankruptcy judge, who will then tell you to suck it up and wait while the issue is sorted out. Demand payment or throw them out, and you will be sitting in the courtroom as a defendant. We were warned, "Leave them be, or you will be fined and possibly put in jail"

Two months went by before the court contacted us and informed us that the bankruptcy case was resolved. They owed no one, and we were advised to work out our differences with the Liars. We were not to ask for any back payment of rent, or face the court's wrath.

Great! So, we had a heart to heart talk with the Liars. This was one of many heart to hearts we had over the years with these delinquents. I was still a naïve person at this point in my life, and I didn't realize that we had been set up. Instead, I thought that these people were going through a rough spot in life, and needed help. I explained that we wouldn't come down on them, and instead, would try to work with them through this. I carefully detailed how we were now stuck with each other, and if they ever hoped to own a home, we were their best shot, as no bank would ever give them a loan for seven years after filing for bankruptcy. It seemed like a good discussion, and I really felt that they appreciated our help and would work hard to make it right.

We laid it on the line for them, and we promised we'd help them get through the bankruptcy if they would focus their resources on paying the rent. We explained that we had a mortgage to pay, and that we could both lose the house if they didn't do their bit.

How did they respond? For the next year, they were late every month with the rent, sometimes taking three to four months to even up. Fact is, they never really evened up with us, but paid us just enough to keep us from evicting them.

At lease renewal time, we asked them to look for another place. We agreed to go month by month while they looked for a new place to live. They put on an academy award performance during this time, complete with lots of crying and promises. Hell, they even got the kids to cry on our shoulders during our meetings. What a terrible thing to do to your kids.

The naïve landlord suckers fell for it, and eventually, we signed a new lease. At least we did make the new lease a month by month deal, with a detailed clause indicating that they would be evicted if they failed to pay even one month's rent. They were late every single month, but threats to throw them out always produced the rent money, in one form or another. Lord knows who they begged or cajoled to get the money month by month.

About six months into the new lease, they had two months in a row of timely payments. We were shell shocked. They indicated that they had their situation resolved, and were now stable. They thanked us profusely for helping them through their rough spell, and continually asked for a full year lease.

After a long discussion, Sandy and I decided to keep the lease on a month by month basis. We could see that this couple was

A Fool's Guide to Landlording

not responsible (as evidenced by new things still showing up in the house on a regular basis), and figured that the pressure of a month by month lease would ensure that we would get paid rent money. Honestly, I wanted these jokers gone, but neither of us had the heart to evict them. Not yet, at least.

So, we went through the same ordeal every month. What a stressful experience to have to pressure people to meet their simple obligations, and all the while live through their personal trials and tribulations. Through it all, they continued to ask for a year lease, which we continued to refuse. Until they pulled their next stunt.

I went away on an international business trip for two weeks. Usually, I informed all of my tenants when I would be gone for long periods so that they knew to call Sandy with any problems. The understanding was that while I was away, they would work through minor problems until I got home. Major problems were to be taken care of by Sandy in the short term. Overall, this strategy worked quite well. Until the Liars started playing the game.

Not long after I left, the Liars called Sandy and told her that I promised to sign a new year lease with them. They told her that I had agreed to this because they were on time with their last few payments. (To them, on time meant that they paid the rent sometime within the month it was due, usually on the last week when I threatened to throw them out.) Semantics, you know.

Poor Sandy couldn't reach me to verify, but knew it was possible that I would agree to this, especially if they were holding up their part of the bargain. She checked our records and determined that the rent was up to date, so she bought their story. On paper, it did look okay, but in reality, this was a very sleazy move on their part.

She had them sign a new one year lease/option deal, and everyone celebrated. The Liars can play the system better than you or me, my friends.

When I got home, Sandy informed me of the progress, and of the deal that was signed. Predictably, I hit the ceiling, and called the Liars to inform them of my displeasure. I warned them to shape up, or this would be their last year in the house. I should've just talked to their dog, for all the good it did.

Once the lease was signed, payments immediately dwindled and stopped. After many meetings and threats, we finally decided to evict these deadbeats. This was our first eviction, and we had much to learn. Of course, the Liars knew much more about this system than we did, and they milked it for all they were worth.

The court is very kind to families with kids, as it should be. It's just in this case, they should take into account the history, which they refuse to do. My goodness, these kids deserved better parents. What hope have they?

After months of court proceedings, we finally forced them to leave. They took it to the very last moment, and we had to have the police stop by to insist that they leave or be thrown in jail. In our area, the police have a set schedule, and they have certain weeks that they perform evictions in certain areas. The Liars even knew when the police were scheduled for our area, and this enabled them to stay to the very last minute. What amazing scum.

So, what did it eventually cost us? How does several thousand dollars grab you? They lived in our house for about six months rent free, and left us with several bills, including the water and sewer. This on top of court costs and lost days of work. The worst part, however, was the mental anguish of dealing with the Liars. The mental cost was astronomical, and fundamentally changed how we viewed human kind. How do you put a cost on that?

In this business, every one lies. It's your job to figure out how big and bad the lies are? You'll probably never see the biggest liars coming, and that's what makes them so dangerous.

A Fool's Guide to Landlording

2. The Losers

The losers took several years off of my life. I'm sure of it. And I'll never forget or forgive them for it.

It all started with a two bedroom house. If you read Chapter 2, you'll soon understand why we gave the advice we did back in that part of the book.

Yep, we were feeling like rental Gods at this point in life. After all, we already had three houses, with three stable tenants, and life was good. We weren't finding any three bedroom houses that met our criteria, so we stumbled onto a couple of nice two bedroom houses, and bought two of them. Well, my wife bought two of them, as I was off in Germany on a business trip. (Our female real estate agent thought I was such an enlightened man for trusting my wife to these decisions on her own. My wife could run circles around most people, so I was actually offended by her comments. I love you Sandy. You go girl!!!)

By the way, the other two-bedroom home turned out to house The Druggies, which is horror story number 3.

Because this house was in better shape, we were able to get it quickly ready to rent. As usual, we had dozens of applicants, and were surprised how many seemed acceptable.

We selected an engaged couple. The man was 35 years old and worked in the restaurant business. The woman was a very young lady (21) who also worked in a restaurant. As it turns out, these two were real losers.

I liked the fact that we would have an older man living in the house, and he assured me that he was mechanically adept. He lied, of course, but how was I to know. It's not like you can make them perform some sort of test, is it? I should've designed some simple experiment, like let's see you fix this leaky faucet, or put together this drain pipe, to see how mechanical they really are.

By the way, if you can rent to someone who has mechanical ability, then you will have far less problems down the road. You want someone who understands the basics of plumbing and electrical systems so that you do not have to run to the house weekly to fix minor annoyances.

As it turned out, these two lied about most things on the application form. For example, they had no intent to lease with option to buy, but knew they wouldn't be accepted if they indicated they just wanted to rent. So, they lied to us about this. And, as it will become clear, neither of them knew a thing about the inner workings of a home, nor did they care. These types of people are a danger to you and themselves, trust me. I never realized how ignorant people can be, even when their ignorance threatens their very livelihood. Wait till you find out all of the stupid things that they did.

Actually, I can't tell you everything, because that would be a book onto itself. So, I'll just hit the highlights, and believe me, you'll have heard enough to keep you laughing for months. In fact, you might accuse me of making this up. But I assure you. Everything here is true. A true nightmare.

Let me tell you a little about the Losers. The 35 year old man had never done much in his life of any consequence, except enlist in the Army for four years. He had no experience, and just drifted through life. At 35 years of age, he was still a busboy for a large restaurant chain. He worked tons of hours, and when home, hooked himself up to video games and played away. The times I tried to have conversations with him, he would only answer in one word sentences, never taking his eyes from the TV screen while he played his games.

The young lady was an attractive ex-cheerleader. Daddy's princess. You know the type, I'm sure. To her credit, she at least worked for a living. She worked behind the counter at a large bagel chain.

They were not married, but engaged. As an interesting side note, only one tenant we ever had consisted of a married couple. Not that this is bad, but it is amazing how many people in this situation are not married. Without being too judgmental, I often wondered if this wasn't a trait that went along with them being

A Fool's Guide to Landlording

irresponsible and non-committal as tenants. Of course, the only married couple I mentioned above was The Liars, so I certainly don't mean to imply that this is a better situation. Just an observation.

The good news was that these particular tenants were responsible enough to pay their rent. In fact, they came from a very luxurious apartment in a fancy suburb of Cleveland where there rent was much higher than what our rent was. I found out later that they were trying to save money for their wedding, so they downgraded to our house from their apartment. Slumming, as it turns out.

To get a clearer picture, their apartment was bigger than the rental house, and had a full list of amenities. A pool, tennis courts, fitness facility, Jacuzzi, club house, the works. They thought our place was a dump, and told me this on several occasions as the months went by. They were slumming to save some dough.

So, upon moving in, their expectations were that I would serve them in a similar fashion to the landlord at a swanky apartment building. Initially, they called me every three days or so complaining about everything known to man. A small crack in an 8 panel windowpane in the rear door. A loose heater vent in the bedroom. Jeeze, I think I even went there to replace a light bulb. I am not joking. I replaced light bulbs for these people.

Good!

So, it began like this. At first, they called wanting a motion sensor light for the detached garage in the back yard. It was too dark, and they were getting scared at night. In reality, I thought this was a reasonable request, so Sandy and I spent a day over there installing the fixture.

To get a feel for this day of work, let me mention that they had two very big dogs. These dogs had an affinity for digging holes in the back yard (and in the house, for that matter: more later). Also, big dogs make big piles, if you know what I mean.

So, after being in the house only 3 weeks, the backyard looked like Beirut, and smelled like a wastewater treatment plant. No, it smelled worse than that, actually.

There had to be 100 holes dug in the small back yard. The holes were about a foot wide, circular, and about one foot deep. Rounded at the bottom of the hole, just like you would expect when paws are your main digging device.

Between the holes were huge piles of dog manure. I don't know what they fed those things, but they should've cut back on the beans. Whew!

The garage had an old power line running to it that had apparently shorted out, and was disconnected from the main power. So, the first order of business was taking down this line and replacing it. By the way, this wire had also been a complaint item. Mr. Handyman was concerned that the line was hanging "too low" and this bothered him. Never mind that it was eight feet above the ground and unpowered. I'll admit, the wire served no useful purpose.

Nevertheless, we took it down and decided to replace it with an underground cable. This meant tapping into the electrical box, running conduit down the side of the house, and digging a trench from the house to the garage and laying wire. Both Sandy and I took turns digging the trench due to a continual gagging reflex. We both nearly threw up dozens of times, as we could barely stomach the stench. You may think I'm kidding, but I am not. It was brutal.

Anyway, the wiring went expertly, and by lunch, we were stringing up the new fixture. We bought a very nice motion detection, double halogen light fixture. It had more options than the Space Shuttle. You could program it every which way but loose. And, it was so bright that it would scare criminals a block away.

We covered up the wiring, checked and rechecked the unit, and called it a day. Our tenants were not home during this time, but were due to come home that night. We left a note asking them

A Fool's Guide to Landlording

to call us and let us know if the lights were working OK. No calls, no nothing.

I called the next day, and they said the light worked fine, and were quite impressed with how bright the lights were. Actually, they complained that they were too bright. Silly me, I was expecting a small "thank you" for getting this installed so quickly and for buying such a nice unit. Instead, they were miffed that it wasn't perfectly what they wanted. Tough, was my thought.

Now it gets funny. So funny I wanted to whack myself with a hammer just to keep my sanity.

Three days later, we get a call complaining about our wiring job. Apparently, the princess called her daddy, who supposedly is also a landlord. (Of course, even he is not stupid enough to rent to his daughter.) Daddy came over, inspected my work, and told his daughter to make me come fix my job because it wasn't to code.

I stopped by, and she proceeded to read me the riot act about our shoddy work. She repeatedly told me the work wasn't to code. When I asked her what the code was, she gave me the most wonderful blank stare. She didn't have a clue.

I explained the Cleveland city code to her for underground outdoor wiring. The work was perfect. Well, it was when I left the day the work was performed. But now, I was seeing something quite different.

You see, one of the dopey dogs apparently took quite an interest in our work. He especially liked the way the conduit from the house went into the ground. Yes, even the fact that it went two feet into the ground before making a 90 degree turn, and continuing on as a buried, outdoor Romax cable. Perfectly legal, and to code, where I live.

But, the damn dog dug a two foot hole right against the house, apparently to inspect if our work was to code.

Instead of apologizing for the damage her dog had done, she proceeded to continue chastising me regarding the security of her animal. She was particularly worried that one of the dumb mutts would bite through the wire and electrocute himself. No such luck, I thought.

I let her finish, as I stood dumbfounded. No thanks for the work, just bitching that I was endangering her animals. I carefully explained that the work was to code, and that I didn't dig the hole, but her damn dog DID. In fact, I told her that I wouldn't fill it in, that she was either to train her dogs to fill in holes, or do it herself. If her dog was so stupid as to bite a live wire, well that was not my problem.

Not only that, but I also told her that she was to fill in all of the holes in the yard, as the yard was beginning to commit suicide.

The holes were filled in 11 months later when they moved out. Only after I threatened to withhold their security deposit.

If you liked that, this story will get so much better for you soon. Again, I'm only hitting the highlights here.

Better!

Next on the agenda was the famous water leak.

The laundry room was located in the mud room next to the back door. The washer and dryer fit snugly against the wall, but still the back door did not clear, and when fully opened, would hit against the washer. No problem, we've all had rooms like this. You expect this in a small house.

One fine Friday evening, Sandy and I returned from a party, and saw we had ten messages on the answering machine. Each message was from The Losers, with each subsequent message increasingly frantic. It seems that a pipe had busted, and they were without a clue as to what to do. It was nearly midnight, but I called over.

A Fool's Guide to Landlording

Before I could get three words out of my mouth, the princess spent ten minutes laying into me about how irresponsible I was. After all, I wasn't at home waiting by the phone for her to call with the latest imperfection in my house. After calming her down, I tentatively asked for the details.

Apparently, of its own accord, the cold water spigot connected to the washer just burst. Water had run everywhere, and the spigot needed to be replaced. Fine. It was late, and I didn't have a spare spigot (again, irresponsible), so I called a plumber, who got right out there the next morning to fix the problem. Bastard charged me $200 to replace a spigot. Chalk that up to another lesson learned.

Anyway, I called the plumber the next day to get the scoop. The spigot had been sheared clean off. There was no evidence of rust (of course it was bronze), and had every appearance of being hit by a blunt object. The water damage appeared fairly substantial, meaning it had run quite some time.

Naturally, I called my tenant and asked if I could come right over to assess the damage.

Upon arriving, I was chastised further about my abilities to be a landlord. I think "shitty landlord" was the operative term used several times. In fact, I was told that things like this don't happen in other people's homes. Apparently, nothing ever breaks in anyone else's homes, just mine.

Well, this is speculation, but this is what I saw. The spigot was indeed sheared clean off. There was a substantial divot in the drywall, apparently caused by the washer being moved. In addition, there was a doorknob shaped divot in the washing machine metal as well. In fact, the divot lined up precisely with the doorknob from the aforementioned back door.

Upon further discussion, it was revealed that one of the idiot dogs came running home to greet the princess and ran straight into the open door just prior to the formal greeting. The washer did indeed move backward, but a subsequent argument ensued that this could have possibly caused the problem. No, my tenants remained steadfast that the pipe just burst of its own accord.

No matter, what's done is done. But it gets better.

Since The Losers are mental midgets, and have never had to live in a place where they ever did anything for themselves, they were not familiar with the inner workings of water lines. It was clear they did not pay attention during our normal tour of the facilities when they moved in. Evidence? They had no clue where the water shutoff valve was. Where was it? You guessed it, right next to the washer.

So, after the pipe magically burst, no one knew how to shut the water off. The princess called the magical Daddy, and he rushed over to help. One hour later he arrived and promptly shut off the water. At least he had some common sense. He found the valve straight away. BUT, the water ran full bore for over an hour while The Losers sat watching, phone firmly in hand, messages sent to my machine every 10 minutes. I'll bet, at some point, they retreated to the living room for gaming activities, but I have no proof of this.

As you might imagine, all of this water did some damage. There is a crawlspace below the laundry room, so the water drained quite well. But not before damaging the dry wall in the room, and the Luan and plywood floor. The floor began to buckle almost immediately.

I was told that the room "needed to be replaced". Today!!! I promised to get the damage fixed, but that it would have to wait until the weekend, so I would have a full two days to fix what was wrong. This did not go over well, so Daddy was summoned to straighten me out.

Daddy wasn't a bad guy, just very protective of the princess. He initially got in my face, screaming at full volume, and telling me what I needed to do. Again, "shitty landlord" was the general gist of the discussion.

A Fool's Guide to Landlording

I responded calmly, which was a surprise to me. I wanted to kill the guy. But I had to handle this, and besides, I wasn't going to let these jerks get to me. After his tirade, I calmly explained that the tenants were partly to blame, and that they would have to be reasonable about the timing of the repair. I also took the opportunity to ask him, why, if he was such the perfect landlord, that he didn't rent his property to his daughter.

He was caught off guard, and stammered repeatedly. Point made. You daughter is a know nothing pain in the ass, and she is living with a pretty worthless specimen of the male species. How could a 35 year old man not know enough to shut off a valve. He also saw the dents in the wall and washer, and probably figured that the tenants did have some complicity in the event at hand. He agreed that the fix could wait until the weekend, and that I was being reasonable in my approach. Frankly, he was relieved that I wasn't pointing fingers.

Sandy and I spent the day tearing down the drywall and replaced a good portion of the floor. With new walls, fresh paint and a new floor, the room looked better than ever. The princess let it be known that she wasn't happy because we awoke her with our hammering and general noise during the tear down. Of course, this work started around 11am, and at noon it became too much for her to sleep. Truth be told, I pounded my hammer extra hard that morning when I arrived and learned she was still sleeping.

She became even more perturbed later in the day, as she had scheduled a little tea party with her friends, and this was also disturbed by our construction sounds. She never so much as offered us a glass of water or something to drink. We went to the local mini-mart whenever we needed something to drink.

Then, lo and behold, she cornered Sandy at the end of the day to ask her, and I quote, "Why does Tony hate me?". Sandy tried to smooth it over and told her that I was just quiet (what a joke to those of you who know me). I wished she asked me, I would've told her exactly what I thought. Especially after slogging through the lovely smells of wet drywall and plywood for an entire day, and busting my ass to put the room back together which The Losers destroyed.

Horror Stories

Pretty bad, huh? I can laugh now, but oh my, at the time.

This was just the warm up for the truly doozy story of The Losers. Can you take anymore? I hope so, because you won't believe this.

I could write a whole book on what they put us through over the next four months. You would be bored to tears, so I'll give you the Reader's Digest version.

The Best!!!!!!

It all started in December, when the weather was getting very cold, and the furnace began running quite a lot. We install Carbon Monoxide detectors in all our houses, in addition to the usual Smoke Alarms. In December, the CO detector went off in the morning, and she panicked and called 911. She vacated the house, while the fire department and the gas company checked the house. By the time they got there, the detector was reading it's normal zero. They cleared her to return to the house. Of course, I received a call, and was threatened with a lawsuit, as they were sure it was the furnace.

It was an old, gravity feed furnace, and of course we were also concerned that this was a possible scenario. I hired an HVAC company to test the furnace out, clean it thoroughly, and get their advice. The furnace was dirty, but now it was clean. The HVAC man said the furnace was fine otherwise, and not to worry. It was a sturdy, old unit with plenty of life in it.

He did say the water heater was old, and could be contributing to the problem, so we had it replaced immediately.

December went by without further incidence. Just a one time anomaly, we thought. We began to believe that perhaps it was the water heater. WRONG!! The fun was just beginning.

Oh, by the way, get used to being threatened with a lawsuit. You will receive this threat on a regular basis, for even the most minor of things. We bought a one million dollar umbrella insurance policy just in case someone tried to bankrupt us, but it was never

A Fool's Guide to Landlording

used, and we were never sued. We never deserved to be sued, it was just a convenient way to threaten us. More later.

So what happened, what happened????

In January, after the holidays, the CO detector went off again. I can't remember the reading, but it was quite high, not the normal zero. By the time help arrived, the meter was back to zero. Something was definitely up, and we needed to solve it.

The detector was located in the hall next to the main bedroom, which was far away from the furnace, but still, the furnace was the lead suspect. The detector went off nearly 4-5 days a week. Always in the morning, and it always awoke The Losers. Honestly, we were quite concerned, and were being threatened with lawsuits constantly.

During the course of the next month or so, we had the gas company out nearly ten times and the fire department out a half dozen times. Each entity did thorough searches of the property with specialized equipment, and neither could find a single thing wrong. We were torn with worry.

One morning, the princess decided to ignore the detector, and pulled the batteries out. She got tired of resetting it. That's funny, let me repeat it. She got tired of resetting the CO detector. Surprise, surprise, she began to get sick after an hour or so, and eventually called 911. They found her still inside, and very pale.

Now, my tenants were truly angry, and the accusations and threats were intensified. More than lawsuits now, we were told that the princess wanted to have a baby some day, and they were sure this was damaging her fertility. They would sue big time for this as well, if we didn't resolve this problem.

We were concerned, and were not sleeping at night at all. Honestly, we were worried about the health and safety of our tenants. I mean, it's bad enough if there was something wrong with the house, but now we had to worry if they would even have the common sense to get out of the house when the detector told them to.

So, we bit the bullet, and hired a HVAC company to put in a new furnace and bought a new gas stove. The HVAC company came in, put in a new furnace (which we took the opportunity to put in air conditioning as well), and replaced the chimney, as this was deteriorating. A new four burner gas stove was introduced to the princess as her reward for her troubles. Many thousands of dollars were spent, but we felt that safety was first.

The next day, the CO detector went off again. I took the day off, and called the gas company. They met me at the house, and we went over the house with a fine toothed comb. Their sensitive detectors gave no reading. After seeing all the money and work we did to the house, they concluded that the gas could not be coming from the house. In their report, they stated that the gas COULD NOT be coming from the house.

I met with the tenants that evening, explained what we had done during the day, and gave them a copy of the report. I was at my wit's end, and I needed them to know that I didn't know what to do. They accused me of conspiring with the gas company to write a false report (like a utility would ever do any favors for the common man). They said I was lying, and that they were talking to their lawyer. I finally asked for their lawyer's name, and, get this, the said they were going to call one of the more popular ambulance chasers that, at the time, appeared regularly on TV. I actually laughed (I know I shouldn't have), but the stress was getting to me. I told them to do what they needed to do, but I was out of ideas.

I left them with the parting shot that they should have their scheister call my lawyer, when convenient.

I offered, as I had since December, to break the lease with no penalties. We could just walk away from each other, and be done. I so wanted them to go. They told me daily how much they hated the house, and how poor a landlord I was. Go, please go. I couldn't have made it more clear. You're not happy here, so please move on. Leave whenever you want, just call me when you're gone. All deposit money refunded. No problems.

Nope, they stayed.

A Fool's Guide to Landlording

Before I left that night, Mr. Loser looked me straight in the eye (I had asked that he stop playing his game for a minute), and told me that I should go home and look at myself in the mirror. Why? Because I would see a man who is shamelessly irresponsible, evil, incompetent and on top of that, a "shitty landlord". I was speechless. After all I have accomplished in my life, this was a surprise. No one had ever had the balls to say this to me.

I nodded my head and bit my tongue. I fought the urge to pounce and pummel, and my brain produced a quick image of me in prison garb. That did the trick. I decided that this piece of crap wasn't worth going to jail over, and I left quietly. No more to say here.

I walked to my car, and I'm embarrassed to say, I actually sat down, closed the door, and cried. Weak and naïve, that's me. I was so frustrated and so hurt by their behavior, and I was so stressed out over the CO situation (which was still unresolved), I couldn't bear to stand it anymore. I only wept for a minute or so, so give me a break all you manly men out there. It felt so good to cry for a moment. Women, back me up here. You know what I am saying.

When I got over my hissy fit, I had an epiphany. I saw it!!!!!! While I was sitting there, this old, crappy, rusty, bucket of bolts pick up truck came down the street, stopped right next to me, and backed into the driveway next door. The truck backed up half way into the driveway, right up to a gate, which was 20 feet in front of the detached garage behind. This placed the truck within a foot of the house, with the back end of the truck right next to the bedroom windows of my house.

A car parked in the garage, the truck parked at the gate. The significance??? The tailpipe of the truck was right next to the main bedroom window.

No way!!! Could this be it??? The pieces fell together instantly.

I got out of the car, and went to the neighbor's house. I didn't know these people from Adam, but they took me in and listened to my story. These are the kind of blue collar folks that great movies are made about. These are the kind of folk that I grew up with, that are my family, that are my friends. My loved ones.

I explained who I was, and the problems I was having with the house and tenants next door. They listened and sympathized. Beers were passed around, toasts were made. When I was done with the story, I asked some questions and they volunteered plenty of information.

Here's what I found. The man gets up every morning, and in the winter, lets the truck run for about 45 minutes to warm up. This way, the truck is nice and warm inside for his drive to work. I offered him ten bucks if I could run his truck for 30-40 minutes the next day, which was his off day. He thought I was crazy to offer him so much money for such a small favor, but he took it. I paid the man, in advance, as is the custom with us folk. We actually shared another beer together and got to know each other. What a truly wonderful night this turned out to be.

During our discussions, his wife laid this bombshell on me. Some days, only in the winter, she also wakes up with very bad headaches. Not every day. Her bedroom is upstairs on the same side as the driveway. Quite likely you could correlate her headaches with the wind direction, in my estimation.

She apparently made this correlation in her own mind, because as I was leaving, I heard her chastising her husband for giving her headaches. A common discussion in most married households, I would imagine.

The next day, I organized a meeting with the gas company. We had become quite close at this point, and I asked the lady from the gas company if she would humor me, and stay with me for a few hours. She happily agreed, as this seemed like a fun way for her to spend a few hours of her day.

I ventured over to the neighbors house, got the truck keys, and started the motor. My gas company lady and me sat inside the house chatting, while her sensor was turned on to monitor CO gas. We sat in the living room, next to the hallway to the bedroom. We sat for half an hour, while the truck ran, and registered no CO gas at all. After a time, we moved into the hallway, and the meter began to pick up a small amount of gas. Finally, after 35 minutes, the meter began to rise substantially. The CO detector went off.

We quickly moved outside, went next to the truck by the bedroom window, and her meter sky rocketed. CO gas was everywhere. And we were outside, in the open air.

Aha!!!!! There it was. The CO gas was not coming from inside, rather it was from the dilapidated old truck.

That explained it. The problem was the truck exhaust, not the furnace, the hot water tank, the stove, or anything inside. That explained why the problem started in the winter months, and ended in spring. The neighbor only had to warm the truck when the weather was cold.

The gas company wrote up a stellar report documenting their findings. The conclusion. The gas came from the truck, not from my house. It seeped in through the windows, and through exterior venting of the crawlspace.

Even though this was a victory for us, the reality was that this was still a bad situation for my tenants. I explained to the neighbor what he was doing by running his truck, and he was mortified. He felt terrible that he was poisoning people. His wife nearly killed him, now that her headache situation was simultaneously solved. In her estimation, this was another example of her husband causing her pain. I asked, and she ordered him to start parking his truck closer to the street, and not next to the house. The problem was solved. Being an engineer, I was proud that I solved a problem that was not intuitive, and difficult, at best, to solve.

I stayed the day to wait for my tenants to come home. I didn't want to rub it in, but I was hoping that they would be relieved that we solved the problem. After all, the gas company lady wrote up a detailed report on the findings, and said, in no uncertain terms, that the cause of the problem was the truck exhaust.

Predictably, The Losers accused me of doctoring the report so that I could avoid responsibility for their discomfort. At this point,

I did not care what they thought. They had done nothing to help us solve this, but rather stood as obstacles to the truth. I left them with a copy of the report, and told them to make sure the neighbor parked his truck in the proper location. I also told them that if they still intended to sue me, I would produce the records of our efforts, and the gas company conclusions, and that I would counter sue them into bankruptcy.

I'd had enough of their attitude. I know that there would be no thanks given, and I didn't want it at this point. On the other hand, if they wanted to pursue this further, and put me through a legal inquisition, I wanted them to know that I would make them pay dearly for their behavior.

They got it!!!!! They tried to pretend to be tough, but the reality is that they never said a word about it to me again. I continued to encourage them to move on, but they stayed. Fact is, they never even bothered to look for a new place until the lease had but 3 weeks left until expiration. Then, to my bewilderment, they asked for an extension to the lease so they could find a place to live. Supposedly, they hated this house, and we were evil. Why would they want to stay??? We let them stay for several weeks, on a week by week basis, so they could find a new home.

You won't believe what they did. They bought a house in a suburb called Lakewood. This is a wonderful suburb of Cleveland, nestled against the lake on the near west side of town. BUT, Lakewood is a very old suburb. Many of the houses are very large, and very old.

They bought a house that was 75 years old. They were so proud of themselves and so happy. It never occurred to them that a 75 year old house might require some maintenance, for which they were incapable of attending to.

I didn't care. They were leaving my life, so I was happy. You should've seen my Academy Award performance on the day they were moving out. I told them both how happy I was for them, and that I wished them well with their new house. I did, honestly. But mostly, I was glad they were leaving.

A Fool's Guide to Landlording

Now tell me, do any of you know of a 75 year old house that won't require any maintenance? No pipes will fail, no electrical problems, no age related problems at all? Of course not. Old houses require maintenance. This is not their strong suite.

Of course, Daddy was there for the big move. He was actually quite friendly to me. No, it's better than that. He pulled me aside and told me that he was amazed how hard we worked to solve the CO problem. He said that my wife and I must be very caring people to be so involved to solve this difficult problem, especially when it turned out not to be our problem at all.

The master landlord even went so far to say that HE, the God, would not have spent all of the money we did to replace all of the equipment in the house we did to solve the problem. No new furnace, no new stove, etc.

Actually, this is a quite a reasonable position. We did go overboard, due to our concerns about the well being of our tenants. For us, it was the right thing to do. No amount of money is worth the peace of mind we attained. Plus, we really believed that our tenants were dangerous. Not dangerous to us, but to themselves. They were so completely incompetent.

They don't belong in a house. They need others to survive. If you won't leave the house when the CO detector tells you that you should, when you let water run for an hour and not look for a way to shut it off, I mean, come on. You're not a danger to society, you're a danger to yourself. I don't need that on my conscience.

On moving day, I warmly greeted and talked to all the family members. I was just so damn happy that they were leaving my life.

Daddy kept wanting to talk to me, perhaps trying to convince me to like his daughter. Uncharacteristically, I was stoic and cold regarding this particular issue. No chance, big guy. Pretty don't mean nice.

Horror Stories

Pack, move, get out. I even helped fill the moving truck. I would've drove the fricking thing to Texas, if I had to.

He actually thanked me, THANKED ME. Yes, he decided, I was a caring man, who while not perfect, did indeed have his daughter's best interest in mind. Fault me if you will, but I couldn't help myself. I had some parting words for Big Daddy. I mean, please, too little, too late. So now I'm OK? I was a shit before, but now I'm OK?? I'm the same man I was before. I care!! You are the one with the problem.

To this day, my wife cannot believe I said this, but I did.

I listened, commiserated, then said to him. "This is the happiest day of my life, Mr. Daddy. Because tomorrow, your daughter is not my charge. I am not responsible for her. When something goes wrong, she will not call me. She will not belittle me. No my friend, tomorrow, when the water line breaks, she can no longer call me to help her. She owns a home now. She owns a 75 year old home now. When, not if, but when something breaks, she will call YOU, not ME!! She is yours now, not mine. Think about that."

He looked at me, and quickly realized the gravity of what I was saying to him. The problems are all his now, not mine. Deal with it big guy. Now you're the bad guy. Reap what you sow.

To be fair, I must close with a minor tidbit. We were not able to give them their full refund of their deposit. Why? Well, they kept their idiot dogs in the bedrooms. One in the front bedroom, one in the back. During the course of their stay, while they were away at work, their idiot dogs (prone to dig holes, as I have mentioned), tried to dig their way out of the bedrooms. Not much damage to the hardwood floor, mind you, but plenty of damage to all of the new carpeting we had put down.

The carpets next to the doors in each bedroom were shredded beyond belief. We asked them to replace the carpets, they refused. Their deposit money helped us to replace the carpeting in each of the bedrooms.

A Fool's Guide to Landlording

I'm sorry to report that this was still at a loss, but at least we only had to spend a fraction of our own money to replace the carpet, and not the whole amount. What with all of the new appliances and rugs, the house sold in a few days. We lost our butt on the sale, but were glad to be done.

I've never lost so much money, and was so grateful at the same time. Life had to get better from here, and it did.

This is gospel. All true. Scared now????

3. The Druggies

Another two bedroom house, another nightmare.

We were attracted to the house because it was a quaint little thing, with an adorable covered back porch on a peaceful street. Apparently, others felt the same, as we had dozens of applicants.

Boy did we get fooled on our number one pick this time. Just goes to show you that our system definitely had its flaws.

We chose a man and woman, mid-40's, unmarried, of course, but seemingly stable. We got on quite well, and they were definitely handy folks. All looked rosy, and we agreed to meet again to sign the lease.

Normally, at the lease signing meeting, we ask for one month's deposit, which goes into the lease option fund for eventual purchase of the home. Everyone is made aware of what is expected at this initial meeting. Bring your money, discuss the lease, set a move in date and sign.

Well, this was the least "smooth" lease signing ever. Our chosen couple showed up brightly and happily on time. They seemed so very excited to be signing on, and just truly loved the house.

After several minutes of pleasantries, we got down to business, and set about the discussion of the lease. This takes about a half hour, the first time through, and all was going spectacularly. Then, just prior to signing, comes the financial portion of the discussion. Time to pay the deposit.

They pulled out two hundred dollars in cash, which was well short of the deposit amount. We sat stunned, and asked what this was about. After all, when we talked on the phone, the amount was discussed and agreed that it would be paid today.

Well, they just didn't have the money, but could get it next week. Yeah, right. They came up with a believable story, and begged their case. We were very reluctant, and very skeptical. They kept talking and talking and talking.

Sandy and I took a break, and went outside to discuss. Indeed, we liked these folks. And, while we had a lot of applicants, we didn't care for many of them personally, and most did not fit all of the requirements that we usually require. The number two choice was significantly less qualified than these folks, on paper, at least.

We decided to take a chance disregarding the advice "No tenant is better than a bad tenant". And this, my friends, was a fateful decision. Remember the advice in Chapter 4, Finding the Ideal Tenant, about re-running the advertisement when your top choices do not pan out? Well, this horror story is one of the reasons that we recommend this approach.

At this time in our rental career, we'd never been through a situation where our top picks failed. And, we didn't want to re-run the ad and go through the application hassle. We still felt that these people would work. We should've thought it through more carefully.

Let's state the obvious here. If your prospective tenants cannot even show up on the day of the lease signing with the proper amount of money, what chance do you think you will have of ever getting rent from these people. If they cannot even do the basics to set a good example, what chaos do you think will ensue.

Of course, this wasn't made obvious until much later. We hope that it is obvious to you now, and that you throw people like this out on their respective ears, should you encounter such a situation.

Say thank you, but no thank you. You have wasted both your time and mine. And, THANK YOU. Yes, thank you. You have just saved me from months of woe by showing your true character right up front.

So, back to the story.

Horror Stories

A few days went by, and they came up with the difference. We started clean and green, and we thought, "Great, we made the right decision. Their sob story was unfortunate, and true, and now we will have no further problems."

We were there on the day they moved in, and we helped them. Then, a month or so later, they needed some work done in the house, and I went over their to do a few repairs and cosmetic fix ups. The rent check came on time in the first month, and the same was true for the second month.

They seemed very pleased, and indicated how much they loved the house. They were happy to have caring landlords, and they loved the lease option arrangement. This would be the house they buy in 3-4 years. Honestly, I still believe that this was their intention. I think their habits got in the way of their dreams.

But, remember, their habits and personal life will become your problems.

On around the third month, problems began to surface. There was an argument, and she left for a few weeks. The rent was late on the fourth month, because she had not returned, and she was helping pay the rent. We worked out a deal to give him some extra time, and he came through again.

So far, each time he told us a story, it seemed to be true, and he would make good on his promises to repay us within a particular time frame. We weren't too worried yet, except we were wondering how he was going to pay the mortgage without her.

Yes, something was beginning to smell. And one of the smells was the strong stench of marijuana on several of the times I went to visit. Mind you, these were not surprise visits, but appointments with the tenant.

This didn't really bother me a lot, as I know there are still a lot of people from the sixties generation that are pot smokers. I would've thought they had grown out of this, but hey, I never considered pot in the same category as more powerful drugs such as Coke, Acid or Heroin. I didn't like it, but I wasn't too worried. But, more about that later.

After a short time, she came back. At the time, he explained to me confidentially that she had a drug problem, and was burning up all the money. That is why he had trouble paying the rent in month 3 and why he "threw her out".

According to him, she begged to come back and promised to clean herself up. She was back, they were happy, the rent got paid for another month or so. What was not to believe? Again, he seemed to have his stuff together to work through what seemed to us to be pretty significant problems.

Shortly after the reunion, things got out of hand. Apparently, there was a very big fight. There was violence, and people were bloodied and bruised. The police were involved. There was a weapon in the house, although thankfully, it was not used or brandished during the incident. But, he went to jail for a weekend, and she was pulling up stakes.

She called me, in tears, and asked me to come over to talk to her. I didn't know what to expect, but was horrified by her description of what was going on. Remember, I had only heard his side of the story. So, I think that she is the weak link here, the unstable one, not him.

Well, she proceeds to tell me what happened on the night in question, and I am aghast at what she is telling me. At first, I am finding it hard to believe. She convinces me by first showing me his stash, then by informing me that he is in jail. I verify this with the police, and now I want to hear the whole story.

First, let me say that even to the end, I liked this guy. He was a stand up guy, who down deep, was a very good man caught in the web of drugs and deceit. He kept trying to clean himself up, but kept falling back.

She echoed this sentiment, and explained that this was why she gave him so many chances. She loved him, and she knew if she could help him, he would be a stellar husband. But, his falls from grace kept getting bigger and bigger.

When she left several months ago, it was because it was the first time he had struck her. Not hard, fortunately, but certainly enough to raise a flag that a new phase in his behavior had begun. Appropriately, she was scared and got the hell out of Dodge.

Apparently, for the next several weeks, he bought her flowers everyday, and apologized profusely. Even he realized that something very bad had happened, and he said he scared himself straight.

She was living with her parents, and they wanted to kill him. But he persevered. He had the guts to go to her parents house, beg to see her, and tell her Dad to take his shots at him to "even up". He promised never to lay a finger on her, and to go straight.

The parents didn't care. They hated him, and threw him out on every occasion. But love being blind, eventually won out. His efforts paid off, and she finally moved back in.

In her words, it was a lovely two weeks. They had romantic dinners. Flowers showed up on a daily basis. His kindness flowed, and she was relieved that his true nature was showing through.

Who knows what happens to people? Who can say what it is that sets them off, and allows their destructive side to take over?

But, somehow, someway, he fell back into the trap.

A few buddies came by to have a "guy's night out". She was reluctant, as she hated his friends, but he had been so good to her, she thought he deserved to have a fun night with his friends. So, this is when the drugs came back home to roost.

He got all tanked up on alcohol and Lord knows what else, and came home. Something happened. She'll never tell. Hell, maybe she doesn't even really know. She claims he was unhappy that she didn't have a meal ready for him to eat (if was 2 am in the morning). Could be, I suppose. Chances are, it could've been anything, but it doesn't really matter, does it? This was a bomb waiting to explode.

This was the night he got very physical, the cops came, and he was whisked off to jail. She informed me that she was taking the opportunity to get out of Dodge for the last time. Would I help?

While I felt terribly sorry for her, I had to say no. I couldn't get in the middle of this. I told her to get some friends, her family, whoever, and get out during the weekend. I'd cover the house for her, and I'd talk to him when he got home. Just leave and don't look back. For safety's sake, if nothing else. And go to a friend's house, not the parents.

She got some help, and was out on a Sunday. He came home on a Monday, and I didn't hear from him for a few days.

At this point, he was about six weeks late on rent, so I used this as a disguise to call him to discuss. He was painfully polite, and invited me over to his house. He said he'd have half the money, with the rest to follow in a few days. Sounded good, and besides, we needed to talk.

I got to his house, and he was, as always, very pleasant. He was honest enough to tell me that he got into a fight with his "old lady", and that he ended up in jail for pissing the cops off. And, he realized that she moved out.

It wasn't hard to notice, mind you, since apparently everything in the house was hers. The place was nearly vacant, and he was upset. He said she stole everything. He said she was a big drug addict, and she screwed him while he was in jail.

Of course, I wasn't buying this anymore, but I sympathized with him in the hope of keeping him in our good graces. After all, he was still my tenant, and we still had to do business. I didn't want him coming after me or Sandy next.

I asked him what he wanted to do. I told him, that under the circumstances, I felt terrible for him, and that he could break his

Horror Stories

lease right now, without any penalty, if he wanted to find a place that he could more easily afford.

He was adamant that he wanted to stay, loved the home, and wanted to buy it as soon as he could. He claimed he made all the money, anyway, and with her gone, he would have more money, as she couldn't steal his money to buy drugs. He gave me the story that he was glad to be rid of her because she was costing him so much money.

Well, I'd heard all this before, but I had to be polite. I told him that we couldn't afford anymore slip ups, and that if he missed rent again, I would begin the eviction process. So, if he ever wanted to buy this house, he'd better straighten up and fly right. It was a heart to heart, and he took it very well. We seemed to have an understanding.

He evened up with the rent in a week, and got himself a whole house of furniture. No doubt, rented, but this was not my concern. My concern was what was going to happen the first of next month.

As expected, the rent did not show up. A week went by, and I called him. There was another story, and this delay was to be lengthy. I gave him a week to pay, or the eviction would be filed.

Just like our first meeting, he called to arrange a meeting and claimed to not only have the money he owed me, but next month's rent; as well, to make up for my inconveniences.

I went to meet him, and he tried to give me the magical $200. As much as I wanted to take his money (as I figured we'd never see another penny), I had already studied the eviction process, and learned that you should never take a partial payment during the eviction process, as it sets a precedent that the court will use against a landlord.

In one of the most heartbreaking meetings of my life, I told him I could not accept a partial payment, and that I would be filing

A Fool's Guide to Landlording

for eviction. He begged, cried and did all but throw himself at my feet. I kid you not.

He followed me to the car, threw himself upon it, and just generally made my heart sink into my stomach. Face it, this business is not for people like us. It is not in our nature to be this cold. But, we couldn't continue like this.

Especially since we were dealing with The Losers and The Liars at the same time. We were going crazy with all these irresponsible people. Not to mention The Derelict, which is the next horror story.

You can read all about the eviction process in Chapter 6, so I'll spare you the details here.

The process went very smoothly in this case, as opposed to when we evicted The Liars.

He showed up for court (which is more than The Liars did), and was there waiting for me prior to the trial. Again, he begged and begged and begged. So polite, so scared.

But, we were committed at that point. You know how you reach a point where you've had enough? You've given enough second chances?

You know the feeling that, even though this is unpleasant, it needs to be done? So, you are right with the world. You have piece of mind.

That's how it was that morning.

We went into the court room, and waited our turn. Our case came up within the first hour, (thankfully), and we both went up to the bench to talk to the judge.

We had all the records (engineers, remember?), so she just read off the charges and asked him if they were true. To our surprise, AND SHOCK, he was truthful to the end. He agreed with all of the charges, and apologized to us and the judge.

She didn't give a wit. She asked if he had kids. Nope. Well then, you have 7 days to get out. Gavel down. Next case.

That was it. Seven days. If you are not out, the police will come help you get out.

He was a prince. He was out in five days, and the place wasn't damaged a bit. What could've been horrible, turned out to be fine. We went into the house, sat down, and let out a huge sigh of relief.

Why are we doing this to ourselves, was the question I remember being asked by both of us?

Get the paint. Let's fix this puppy up, clean it, and put in on the market.

Once again, the house attracted people like flies, and it sold in just a few weeks. We decided that we liked the feeling of off loading the houses, and began to make plans to exit the business, and get our nice, dull little lives back.

4 The Derelict

The Derelict was a young man about 20 years old. He was serious and seemed so very responsible for his age.

He rose to the top of our list for so many reasons. He owned his own roofing business. He intended to make significant enhancements to the home, and would eventually be buying it. In fact, he offered to give us $10,000 to hold in our option fund for eventual purchase of the home.

Silly us, we told him that we didn't need to put that much money in, and that he could hang on to it until he was ready to buy the house. Wouldn't do that again. Take the money, next time. If nothing else, for security and leverage.

We made a mistake from the start with this house. First, we strayed from our business model. We found what appeared to be a steal in a nearby suburb. We had no experience in these neighborhoods, and while the house was a good deal, it was significantly more expensive than our other homes. This meant that the rent would be higher than previous homes.

We learned that rents in this range are hard to get.

Because of this, we had very few qualified applicants. The Derelict wasn't even our number one. He was number three, but number one and two backed out. So, we decided to meet with The Derelict and discuss matters.

Oh, by the way, we didn't commit the same error as we did with The Druggies. We actually re-ran the ad three or four times. So, at least we were smart enough to keep trying, and not just take the number three guy from the first application pile.

No, The Derelict came along on the third try, I think. So, we even tried advertising again just to see if we could find someone better than The Derelict.

No dice. It was him or nobody. And the house had been vacant for about two months now, so we needed to do something.

Horror Stories

We took another unusual step. We set up a second interview with The Derelict. This meeting was not the usual lease signing meeting, it was a second interview.

We told him we were concerned whether he would meet his commitments, what with being so young and inexperienced. This was an older house, and we needed to make sure he could handle it. Also, we were trying to find out more about him, his finances, etc.

We found out a bunch. He really was a roofer, and this guy made gobs of cash. And, I do mean cash. He always had a wad of money bigger than I've ever seen, and everything was bought with the green stuff.

His Dad was in jail, so he was on his own. So, he decided he was going to get his life together early and be rich. Lord knows what this poor kid had to see during his short life. It scared him straight, I can tell you that.

So, that was the idea behind the business. That was the idea behind owning a home. The Derelict wanted to be a successful businessman who would never be looked down upon by society. He had cleaned up his act, and was asking for a chance. Again, the offer for up front money was made. He promised to buy the house in three years, assuming he liked living there. So, perhaps you can see this one coming like a freight train.

While a sad story, he was very sincere and he really did want to make good. We thanked him for his candidness, and promised to get back to him soon.

Sandy and I talked about him for days. What to do, what to do? What a risk, but what a wonderful thing it would be if we helped and all turned out well. Our hearts won again, and the fun began. But, so you don't think you'll be bored, this is not the same fun as the other stories. This one is just different.

It all started magnificently. The rent was paid timely, and required a visit, as it was paid in cash (of course). Considering the problems with other tenants, I never minded this. This house was close to our own home. And, so far, The Derelict was very responsible.

He bought a house full of furniture, all top quality. Leather couches, big screen, etc. The house was just beautiful inside.

On several visits to collect rent, this house also had the unmistakable odor of pot. In fact, there were always several young men and women in the living room when I visited, and on a few occasions I would see someone run out of the living room into the bedroom. To this day, I figure this was the one holding the joint, but who knows.

Again, I didn't care too much about the pot. But I was very careful with this one, because he seemed to me to be the type that was into much more than pot.

To be fair, we never had a rent problem with this tenant. That is why I said before that this story is different. He paid his rent every month, and we had him as a tenant for two years.

In fact, the first year wasn't too terribly bad. He was stable, and while not real personable, a decent enough person to talk to. He liked us and we liked him. He asked for very little the first year, but we were there for him on every occasion.

The house had a large two and a half car garage. He was buying motorcycles and other expensive stuff (a boat), and the garage door was pretty crappy. He asked for a new one, and we bought it. $1000 expense, but he had a good point.

We were so chummy, that we even contracted his company to re-roof another one of our rental houses. By the way, no matter how good this sounds, never do business with your tenants. It's like the advice that you should never do business with your family. It all sounds so good on the surface, but should anything go wrong, you can really cause a lot of damage to relationships.

That didn't really happen in this case, but all was not well. He was clearly a good roofer, but it had been raining a lot, and I didn't like how long he was taking to do the job. Neither did The

Liars, who were giving him a really tough time. The Liars were probably the reason he didn't like going over there.

Never mind that, though, you have a job to do. Most times I've seen a roof done, it is a couple of day ordeal. This is what I expected.

But no, The Derelict goes over to the house, peels off the old roof, and finds some damaged plywood. No problem, I tell him to replace what he has to, and I'll pay for it. He begins to do this, and The Liars begin to give him a hard time that he is leaving gaps in the roof, and that the boards are not straight.

I have to inspect. Indeed, he is leaving a hole in the roof, that while it will be OK when shingled, really should be filled in. As for the "bumpiness" in the plywood, that is the nature of the beast, and you'll hardly see it with the shingles.

So, I go to his house to explain the compromise. He gets totally pissed off, and the house sits for a week with no roof. The Liars are calling me every hour, and The Derelict won't answer or return my phone calls.

Worse yet, the rain is beating down on the exposed plywood, and some is getting into the house.

I don't remember how, but this got resolved in the next week or so, and the house was finished up in a total of three weeks. It looked fine, but our relationship with The Derelict had begun a new phase.

Plus, he had changed. Part of the reason that the roof took so long is that he was sleeping off some binge or another. You could tell something was up, because he was very moody now, and clearly slipping back into whatever life style he was living before.

Our discussions got more intense over the next few months. Mostly over roofing issues.

We had promised him that we would pay him for a new roof on the house he was living in when we signed the second year lease.

A Fool's Guide to Landlording

Sandy was opposed to this, as she pointed out that he wanted to buy the house in another year, but expected us to give him a new roof. It wasn't clear that the old roof needed replacement.

However, he intended to walk away from the house if we didn't do this, so I pushed to let him do it. I wanted him to buy the house.

So, we agreed that he could do the roof, but I put in stipulations based on our previous track record with roofing and The Derelict. I put in writing that he was to do the roof in the summer months, and take just three days to do it.

The summer passed slowly as I continually reminded him that he would have to do it soon, or not at all. He huffed and puffed. Summer came and went, and no roof. I warned him that his opportunity was fading. He just swore at me.

I let the subject drop, as I was tired of the fighting.

Finally, in December, with all the snow and sleet, he calls to inform me that he will be starting the roof. I absolutely forbid this, and we get into a big fight on the phone. He tells me to get my butt over to his place to discuss, because he has a thing or two to tell me. He is clearly drugged up.

I try to push the meeting off, but he tells me that he knows where I live, and he'll be coming over.

No, no, no!!!! Stop right there. We can meet, just not at my house or yours. But, Sandy is out of town, and I don't want to go without someone knowing where I am. I tell him that I will meet him at a local Wendy's, and that I'll buy him lunch so we can cool down. I just want a nice PUBLIC place so I don't get killed.

You might think that I am being paranoid. But you don't know this guy, and I'm sure he is armed. I'm sure he can kill. He had become so violent and unstable over the past few months. He was heavily into drugs, you could see it in his eyes and his demeanor.

I called my Mom and explained what was happening. I told her that I would call her at specified times over the next two hours, and that if I didn't call within 5 minutes of the specified times, she was to call the police and tell them of our whereabouts. She panicked, but said she would do her part.

I met him at the Wendy's. He came in like a tornado, ready to rock. I told him to sit down. I asked him what he wanted, ordered the food, and sat across from him. Calmly, I told him that I didn't want to make a scene, and that I had several people that were informed of what was going on, and that they were backing me up. Once false move, and the cops would be hauling him away.

I told him that I suspected him of drugs, and that I suspected he had a weapon on his person. Even if he succeeded in hurting me, the cops would be on him before he could get out of the door.

There it was, I was waiting on the edge of my seat for the explosion. Lord help me, the pressure worked. He sat back, sighed, looked me in the eye and said he was sorry. Told me he was SORRY!!!!!

I didn't have to say anymore, he took the conversation from there. He told me that he had screwed up, and was too high to get the roof done in the summer. But, he needed the money now, and that was why he wanted the work. He apologized, and agreed that December was not a good time. His lease was done in January, and he said he needed to move on. I agreed. We ate lunch in silence, and I went to a pay phone to make one of the appointed phone calls.

Mom was relieved. Well, yeah Mom, so was I. I fully expected to be shot or maimed that day. Now, I was getting rid of him in two months. What a joy.

He was more respectful to me than ever for the next two months. He paid his rent on time (he always did), and he moved out without a problem. He was GONE, baby, GONE.

Once he left, I went to look the house over. It was clean and in good shape. Everything had been moved out, and the place

A Fool's Guide to Landlording

looked pretty good. I checked all of the cabinets and closets, and I saw the strangest sight in the hall closet. This was a closet made with several shelves. It was used as a pantry and general storage area. On the eye level shelf was a clip from a gun.

I'm not a gun guy, so I couldn't tell you what make or model. But, the clip was full of bullets. And there it sat, right at eye level for me to find. A message? You tell me.

While we were doing the routine cleaning, the next door neighbors came over to see what we were up to. They were a friendly couple who we had met and had dinner with on one occasion when we were first fixing the house up several years ago.

She was a dispatcher for the police in this suburb, and he was a police officer. Nice folks.

Anyway, she proceeded to tell me about The Derelict. Apparently, he had quite a long "sheet" on him at the local police station. In fact, for the past several months the house was on "watch", as the police suspected that it was being used as a drug house.

As you might expect, our police friends were glad to see The Derelict go. They told me that this was a BAD, BAD apple. When I told them about my Wendy's story, they told me that I was lucky to get out alive. Smart move to meet in public, as he feared jail more than anything.

They believe to this day that he would've taken a different course of action if I had met him at his house, as he had asked. Probably would've planted a garden, with me as fertilizer.

As luck would have it, we ran into him at a local bar several months later, and he commented on how we hadn't sold the house yet. We hadn't, and I didn't appreciate that he was keeping tabs. It took months to sell that white elephant.

He was pleasant, but creepy. He made mention of the fact that we had moved.

Horror Stories

Indeed, we had just moved into a new house ourselves, but how the hell did he know that. He just smiled and said he had to go. My heart sank, yet again. Was this crazy bastard a part of our life now?

That was seven years ago, and I've never heard from him again. Thank God. He's probably in jail, and that is probably our saving grace.

See how rentals spice up your life? It's the gift that just keeps giving.

A Fool's Guide to Landlording
5 The Almost Winners

Hands down, the best tenants we ever had were our first tenants. But, these are the types of folk who live their lives "snatching defeat from the jaws of victory".

To this day, I wish that our first tenants had been awful. Had they been awful, we would've stopped right there, and had only one bad experience to learn from.

But Nooo, they had to be model citizens, and thus give us the false impression that we could make a go of our business model. In fact, they reinforced the impression that our approach was sound. If followed, this approach would produce a good match between house and tenant, and would be beneficial for all.

Of course, this is not meant to point blame at them. To the contrary, they were the nicest couple we ever rented to, and it is a shame that the end of this story is not a happy one for them. This is more their horror story, than ours.

We were brand new to the game of rental houses. We had just bought a three bedroom, slab home in the West Park neighborhood of Cleveland. The area was wonderful, and we paid just a little below market value for the house, as it was in quite good shape.

For our first foray into the business, we wanted to keep it simple. Once we learned some skills, we could (and would) take on greater challenges.

So, a new coat of paint, a little carpeting, and this puppy was ready to rent.

We must've had 50 applicants in one weekend's open house. At least 10 of these folks met the criteria we were looking for. The top three were all marvelous. The Almost Winners were number One by a long shot.

Good income, great people, handyman in the family, motivated and wanted to own their own home. We signed them on, and they moved in right away. He was self employed in a trade business, and she was in school.

From the start, he began fixing the place up to their style. And, oh my, what a wonderful style it was. These folks were so good with their hands, and so creative. Within a month or so, the house had a new décor inside, and looked like something you see in Better Homes and Gardens.

We talked regularly with these folks, and even had dinner with them a few times. They were just enjoyable company.

She was very sweet, but very spastic. He was a rock of Gibraltar type guy, with a natural kindness. They were a match made in heaven. She gave him the excitement of impulsiveness and he provided calm when she would go ballistic.

I admired him, frankly. He had his hands full keeping the emotions at bay in that house. He was someone that wasn't happy unless he was doing something. After he got done painting and decorating the living room and kitchen, he started on the bath. He put in a shower surround (which we helped pay for), and put ceramic tile down in the bathroom.

Then, he discovered that there was an old brick patio next to the garage that had been buried. He dug it up, cleaned and had himself a spectacular patio in a garden like setting. He completed the look by putting a wire frame table complete with Cinzano Vino umbrella. You know the look. Everyone loves that, "Italian garden look", don't they?

So, things were just grand. They paid their rent every month, and whenever he wanted or needed something, we were happy to give it. He had put so much love and attention into this little house.

They lived in the house three and a half years. We kept the rent the same, and would've kept it the same for as long as we could. (This is our normal policy for good tenants, as discussed in Chapter 7.)

A Fool's Guide to Landlording

I was positive that they would buy the house. They were positive that they would buy the house. In the middle of the third year, we began discussing how at the end of the lease, they would have enough down payment money saved up in the option account to buy the house. We were getting ready to do the deal.

In July, with just six months to go, we received a call from the lord of the manor. I expected him to tell me to get the paperwork moving, because they were ready. By the tone of his voice, I quickly realized that something far worse was happening.

He was somber, and told me that he had some serious problems. He and his girlfriend had been together 8 years and she had left him for another man.

Apparently, she had been fooling around on him for a year, but waited until he paid for the last of her schooling to make her announcement. And now, she was gone. He was heartbroken.

After all of her emotional shenanigans, he was left holding the bag. He needed our help. He couldn't honor the last six months of the lease. BUT, he promised to pay rent until we could find another tenant.

No dice. He had been such a great tenant, and he was clearly hurting so badly now, we told him that we would break the lease at his discretion, and refund the whole deposit. He needed some friends. We told him to think it through, and let us know when he needed to leave.

He called back the next day, and said he'd leave in a week. This would've put him two weeks into the month, but we told him to move when convenient, and not worry about the two weeks of rent. Get yourself settled, and let us know when we can have the keys back. He was so grateful, I can't tell you. He openly wept on the phone.

You see, life was even worse for him than just the girlfriend leaving. His accountant friend had given him bad advice on taxes, so apparently the IRS was causing him great grief as well.

Grief to the tune of $12,000 in back taxes, complete with a threat of fines and jail time.

He was a good guy, and somebody really steered him wrong. So now, he had this monkey on his back as well.

To this day, we feel awful for him. The Almost Winners. Just when they're set to succeed, they make major life altering mistakes that sets them back years in their lives.

It's unfortunate, but these are just another of the types of folks who you will encounter in this business.

Chapter 10

Conclusions

Of all the information and advice contained in this book, the most important we can offer is to take your time to do your homework. The headaches and heartaches that come with the responsibility of being a landlord can make your life miserable. Yes, perhaps a sense of accomplishment for a job well done, some money in the bank and appreciating property. However, the downside may be dark and not worth the investment in money and time. Make contacts with various banks about financing options. Try to meet other people who are already landlords and get information on what communities offer good potential for investments. Travel the potential neighborhoods during the day and evening hours. And read, read, read any information you can find on the subject. On legal matters, contact your attorney. For financial issue, contact an accountant. Contract out any repairs that you are not qualified to perform or that require 'qualified professionals' perform as part of your local codes. We wish you the best of luck.

Chapter 11

Sources of Additional Information

1. Bierbrier, Doreen, "Living with Tenants: How to Happily Share your house with renters for Security and Profit", McGraw-Hill, 1986.
2. Daniel Goodwin and Richard Rusdorf, "The Landlord's Handbook: A complete guide to managing small residential properties", Real Estate Education Company, 1998.
3. Bierbrier, Doreen, "Managing your Rental House for Increased Income", McGraw-Hill, 1985.
4. Robert Irwin, "The Landlord's Troubleshooter" 2nd Edition, Dearborn Financial Publishing, Inc., 1999.
5. Jeffery Taylor, "The Landlord's Kit", Dearborn Trade Publishing, 2002.
6. Leigh Robinson, "Landlording", Express, 2001.

Appendix I: Sample Application Form

CONFIDENTIAL LEASE APPLICATION

Applicant Name (Please Print) _____ DL #: _____

Date of Birth _____ SS # _____ Home Phone # _____

Present Address _____

How Long? _____ Present rent or mortgage $ _____ /month
If less than four years, please list previous addresses on the back of this application.

Name of Landlord _____ Phone # _____

Applicant Employed by: _____

How Long _____ Work Phone _____

Work Address _____

Position _____ Monthly Salary $ _____ /month
If employed at this company two years or less, provide same information on previous employer on back of application.

Co-Applicant/Spouses Name _____ DL # _____

Date of Birth _____ SS # _____ Home Phone # _____

Co-Applicant Employed by: _____

How Long _____ Work Phone _____

Work Address _____

Position _____ Monthly Salary $ _____ /month
If employed at this company two years or less, provide same information on previous employer on back of application.

Total number of persons to occupy residence _____ Total number of children _____

# of pets _____ Type of pets _____ Desired move in date: _____

Are you interested in the option of leasing this house to own it? (Lease option) _____

Have you ever been evicted before? _____

Checking account bank and number _____

Savings account bank and number _____

Total outstanding debt _____ Monthly payment toward debts? _____
(car payments, credit card bills, student loans, medical bills, etc.)

I hearby certify that the above information is truthful and accurate. I hearby authorize the person to whom this application is made to investigate the above information and statements pertaining to my credit and financial responsibility.

PLEASE READ THE STATEMENT ABOVE BEFORE SIGNING THE APPLICATION

Applicant Signature _____ Date: _____

Applicant Signature _____ Date: _____

Appendix II: Sample Lease with Option to Buy Agreement

RESIDENTIAL LEASE WITH OPTION TO PURCHASE AGREEMENT

THIS AGREEMENT is made _____ by and between

who with _____ heirs, executors, administrators and assigns, are hereinafter called the "Lessor/Seller", and

who with _____ heirs, executors, administrators and assigns, are hereinafter called the "Lessee/Buyer".

1. **SUBJECT PROPERTY:** Lessor/Seller does hereby let and lease unto the Lessee/Buyer the Property located at

in the County of _____ and State of _____ together with all its improvements including the following non-real estate items _____ hereafter referred to as the "Property."

2. **TERM:** The term of this lease shall be for a period of _____, commencing on _____ and ending on _____. This lease shall automatically renew on a month-to-month basis upon the same terms and conditions unless either party provides written notice of termination to the other party at least thirty (30) days before the end of the lease term or unless another lease is signed by both parties

3. **RENT:** Lessee/Buyer agrees to pay Lessor/Seller as rent for the Property during the the term, the sum of _____ ($_____) per month, payable in advance and without demand, deduction, or offset (except as specifically provided to the contrary in this lease) in equal monthly payments of $_____ ON OR BEFORE THE FIRST (1ST) DAY OF EACH CALENDAR MONTH and continuing thereafter until Lessee/Buyer has paid the total sum. Lessee/Buyer shall make all rents payable to _____ at _____ or at such other place that Lessor/Seller may designate from time to time in writing. The prorated rent from the commencement date of this lease to the first (1st) day of the following month is $_____. The prorated rent is due on or before the _____ day of _____, _____. Lessee/Buyer's failure to pay monthly rent in accordance with the terms of this lease is a default of this lease. Lessor/Seller shall apply all monies received from Lessee/Buyer first to non-rent obligations of Lessee/Buyer including late charges and returned check charges, repairs, brokerage fees, and periodic utilities, if any, then to rent regardless of any notations on a check. Lessor/Seller may report unpaid rent, charges or damages to credit reporting agencies. Any additional money owed to Lessor/Seller due to previously stated reasons shall be deducted from the option money amount if prompt payment is not rendered. Lessee/Buyer shall pay any non-mandatory fees for use of any common areas or facilities (such as pool or tennis courts) managed or owned by a homeowner or neighborhood association.

4. **RENT INCREASES:** There shall be no rent increases during the term of this lease. If this lease is renewed automatically on a month-to-month basis, Lessor/Seller may increase the rent during the renewal period at will by providing written notice to Lessee/Buyer at least thirty (30) days prior to the effective date of the increase in rent.

5. **LATE CHARGES:** If all rent is not paid on or before the _____ day of the month, Lessee/Buyer agrees to pay a late charge of $_____ plus a further late charge of $_____ per day thereafter until rent is paid in full as liquidated damages for Lessor/Seller's inconvenience and time in collecting late rent. Daily late charge shall not exceed thirty (30) days for any one month. Lessor/Seller and Lessee/Buyer agree that it is difficult to determine the exact amount of expenses or damages which Lessor/Seller may incur in collecting late rent and further agree that the amount of the late charges specified in this paragraph is reasonable to compensate Lessor/Seller or Lessor/Seller's expenses, time, and inconvenience in collecting late rent as liquidated damages.

6. **RETURNED CHECKS:** *Lessee/Buyer shall pay a fee of $_____ (not to exceed $25) for each check Lessee/Buyer tenders to Lessor/Seller which is returned by the institution on which it is drawn for any reason, plus initial and additional late charges until Lessor/Seller has received payment. Lessor/Seller, by providing written notice to Lessee/Buyer, may require Lessee/Buyer to pay all amounts due by this lease in cash, cashier's check, certified check, or money order.*

7. **OPTION TO PURCHASE:**

    (a) Lessor/Seller grants to Lessee/Buyer, subject to the provisions of Paragraphs 20 and 21, the right to purchase at any time during the time period of _____ through _____ the Property for the amount of _____ Dollars ($_____) conditioned upon full compliance by Lessee/Buyer with all terms of this Agreement.

    (b) Lessee/Buyer agrees to pay $_____ to Lessor/Seller as consideration for Lessor/Seller granting Lessee/Buyer an option to purchase the Property. This consideration shall be paid as follows: $_____ prior to occupancy and $_____ per month which is included in the monthly rent as stated in Paragraph 3. Lessor/Seller agrees that upon exercise of the option, Lessee/Buyer shall be credited with $_____ from each monthly rental payment plus the initial $_____ option consideration paid prior to occupancy. **SHOULD OPTION NOT BE EXERCISED BY LESSEE/BUYER, THERE WILL BE NO REFUND OF ANY OPTION CONSIDERATION.**

8. **NOTICE OF TERMINATION:**

    (a) <u>*Lessee/Buyer shall provide Lessor/Seller written notice of Lessee/Buyer's intent to vacate and terminate this lease at least thirty (30) days prior to the termination date or the end of any renewal period of this lease or this lease shall automatically renew on a month-to-month basis.*</u> *VERBAL NOTICE IS NOT SUFFICIENT UNDER ANY CIRCUMSTANCES. If this lease is automatically renewed on a month-to-month basis either party may terminate the renewal of this lease by providing written notice to the other party which states that the renewal of this lease shall terminate on the date designated in the notice but not sooner than thirty (30) days after the date the notice is given.*

    (b) Lessee/Buyer shall deliver up and surrender to the Lessor/Seller, possession of the Property hereby leased upon at the expiration of this lease, or its termination in any way, or if option is not exercised and lease is not extended, in as good condition and repair as when received (normal wear and tear excepted) and deliver the keys to Lessor/Seller of the Property. Normal wear and tear shall mean deterioration which occurs without negligence, carelessness, accident, or abuse.

9. **OCCUPANCY:**

    (a) Lessee/Buyer shall use the Property as a private dwelling only. Lessee/Buyer agrees that the Property shall be occupied by no more that _____ persons, consisting of _____ adults and _____ person(s) under the age of 18, without written consent of Lessor/Seller.

    (b) Lessee/Buyer shall not permit any guest to stay in the Property longer than ten (10) days without Lessor/Seller's written permission, otherwise, Lessee/Buyer shall be in default of this lease.

    (c) Lessee/Buyer agrees that the Property shall be occupied by no more than _____ domestic animals, specifically _____, without written consent of Lessor/Seller. If Lessee/Buyer violates the pet restrictions of this lease, Lessee/Buyer shall pay Lessor/Seller a fee of $_____ per day for each day Lessee/Buyer violates the pet restrictions as additional rent for any unauthorized pet. Lessor/Seller may remove or cause to be removed any unauthorized pet and deliver any unauthorized pet to appropriate local authorities or request local authorities to remove any unauthorized pet by providing written notice to Lessee/Buyer of Lessor/Seller's intention to remove or cause any unauthorized pet to be removed. Lessee/Buyer agrees that Lessor/Seller shall not be liable for any harm, injury, death, or sickness to any unauthorized pet provided Lessor/Seller has used reasonable and humane means to remove or cause any unauthorized pet to be removed. Lessee/Buyer shall be responsible and liable for any damage to the Property or to others caused by any unauthorized pet and for all costs Lessor/Seller may incur in removing or causing any unauthorized pet to be removed.

10. **USE OF PROPERTY:** *Lessee/Buyer shall not permit the Property or any part of the Property to be used for: (a) any activity which is offensive, noisy, or dangerous, or otherwise constitutes a nuisance; (b) the repair of any vehicle; (c) any business of any type, including child care, unless otherwise agreed in writing; (d) any activity which violates any applicable deed, homeowner association, or subdivision restriction; or (e) any illegal or unlawful activity or other activity which shall obstruct, interfere with, or infringe on the rights of other persons near the Property. Lessor/Seller hereby agrees that if the Lessee/Buyer performs all the covenants and agreements herein stipulated to be performed on Lessee/Buyer's part, the Lessee/Buyer shall at all times during the term have the peaceable and quiet enjoyment and possession of the Property without any manner of let or hindrance from Lessor/Seller or any person or persons lawfully claiming the Property.*

11. UTILITIES: Lessee/Buyer shall pay (in addition to the rents herein specified) all water, sewer, gas, electricity, garbage, telephone, alarm monitoring systems, and cable television rents levied or charged against the Property for and during the term for which this lease is granted. In case no water rents are levied or charged specifically against the Property, Lessee/Buyer shall pay to Lessor/Seller water rent at city rates for the amount of water registered during the term of this lease by the re-registering meter connected with the water pipes supplying the Property. In case any such water rent is not paid by Lessee/Buyer at the time when water rent is payable to the proper city officials, Lessor/Seller may nevertheless pay the same to such officials. Any amounts so paid by Lessor/Seller and any amounts paid by Lessor/Seller to keep the Property in a clean, safe, and healthy condition as herein before specified, or to make up any default on Lessee/Buyer's part to fulfill Lessee/Buyer's covenants herein written, are hereby agreed and declared to be so much additional rent and shall be due and payable with the next installment of rent due thereafter under this lease.

12. INSURANCE: Lessor/Seller shall maintain a policy of fire insurance in the amount of at least $_____ insuring the Property from loss by fire or other disaster during the lease period and to close of escrow. Any loss to the real property or personal property (exclusive of Lessee/Buyer's furnishings and personal belongings) contained therein for any reason whatsoever, including condemnation by any governmental agency, fire, flood, or whatever, which is not covered by Lessor/Seller's policy of insurance, shall be apportioned between the parties as to their interests pursuant to this agreement.

13. VEHICLES: Lessee/Buyer shall not permit more than _____ vehicles (including but not limited to automobiles, trucks, recreational vehicles, trailers, motorcycles, and boats) on the Property unless authorized by Lessor/Seller in writing. Lessee/Buyer shall not park any vehicles in the yard as defined in paragraph 19. Lessee/Buyer shall not store any vehicles on or adjacent to the Property or on the street in front of the Property. Lessor/Seller may tow, at Lessee/Buyer's expense, any improperly parked or inoperative vehicle on or adjacent to the Property in accordance with applicable state and local laws.

14. ACCESS BY LESSOR/SELLER: Lessor/Seller or anyone authorized by Lessor/Seller may enter the Property by reasonable means at reasonable times without notice to: (a) inspect the Property for condition; (b) make repairs; (c) show the Property to prospective tenants, purchasers, governmental inspectors, fire marshals, lenders, appraisers, or insurance agents; (d) leave written notices; or (e) seize nonexempt property after an event of default. Lessor/Seller may prominently display a "For Sale" or "For Lease" or similarly worded sign on the Property within ninety (90) days of the expiration of this lease or any renewal period.

15. MOVE-IN CONDITION: Lessee/Buyer has inspected and accepts the Property AS-IS except for conditions materially affecting the safety or health of ordinary persons or unless expressly noted otherwise in this lease. Lessor/Seller has made no express or implied warranties as to the condition of the Property and no agreements have been made regarding future repairs unless specified in this lease. Lessee/Buyer shall notify Lessor/Seller in writing of any defects or damages to the Property, and deliver it to the Lessor/Seller within 48 hours after the commencement date of this lease. Lessee/Buyer's failure to timely deliver any written notice of defect and damage shall be deemed as Lessee/Buyer's acceptance of the Property in a clean and good condition.

16. REPAIRS AND RESPONSIBILITY FOR PROPERTY CONDITION:

(a) *Lessee/Buyer's General Responsibilities:* Lessee/Buyer shall keep the Property, including all rooms, bathrooms, and appliances, clean and sanitary. Lessee/Buyer shall dispose of garbage only in appropriate receptacles. Lessee/Buyer shall use reasonable diligence in the care of the Property and at Lessee/Buyer's expense shall be responsible for: (i) costs of plumbing stoppages and damages caused by foreign or improper objects not caused by Lessor/Seller's negligence in lines exclusively serving the Property; (ii) damages to doors, windows, or screens not caused by Lessor/Seller's negligence; (iii) damages from windows or doors left open; (iv) supplying and changing heating and air conditioning filters at monthly intervals; (v) supplying and replacing light bulbs and smoke detector batteries; (vi) replacement of yard or shrubbery caused by Lessee/Buyer's negligence; (vii) prompt removal of trash from the Property; (viii) eliminating any condition dangerous to health and safety caused by Lessee/Buyer or Lessee/Buyer's guests; (ix) cost of pest control; (x) taking precautions to preclude broken water pipes due to freezing; and (xi) lost or misplaced keys and garage door openers. LESSEE/BUYER'S FAILURE TO MAINTAIN PROPERTY OR PROMPTLY NOTIFY LESSOR/SELLER SHALL MAKE LESSEE/BUYER RESPONSIBLE FOR ALL RESULTING REPAIRS.

(b) *Repairs:* Lessor/Seller is NOT obligated to repair or remedy a condition caused by Lessee/Buyer, or lawful occupant, member of Lessee/Buyer's family, or guest of Lessee/Buyer unless the condition was caused by normal wear and tear. Lessor/Seller may temporarily interrupt utilities and use of any fixture or appliance in order to complete repairs, construction, or remedy an emergency, and the amount of the rent shall not be adjusted or reduced to accommodate for the interruption. Lessor/Seller shall act with due diligence in completing any repair but shall not be obligated to make repairs on a day other than a business day except in the case of emergency. For the purposes of the lease, "emergency" means a problem that materially affects the health or safety of an ordinary tenant and is not a condition that merely causes inconvenience or discomfort. Except as otherwise agreed in this lease and except for those repairs caused by fire, interruption of utilities, or other emergency, Lessee/Buyer shall cause to be repaired and pay the full cost of any repair to the Property provided the cost of any such repair does not exceed $_____ per each occurrence. *Lessee/Buyer shall cause any repair to be made only by qualified repairmen, technicians, or professionals. Lessee/Buyer shall not repair or attempt to repair any item by Lessee/Buyer's self. If repairs exceed the stated amount, Lessee/Buyer shall direct all requests for repairs to Lessor/Seller in writing and all expenses over and above the stated amount shall be shared equally by Lessee/Buyer and Lessor/Seller. Both parties acknowledge that the rent would be higher if the foregoing responsibilities were allocated differently. This assumption of responsibility by Lessee/Buyer is entered into knowingly, voluntarily, and for consideration and is an express waiver of any statutory or common law obligation of Lessor/Seller.*

(c) *Prohibited Acts By Lessee/Buyer:* Lessee/Buyer shall NOT, unless Lessor/Seller provides written permission to: (i) remove any part of the Property or any of Lessor/Seller's personal property for any purpose; (ii) remove, change, or re-key any lock; (iii) make holes in the woodwork, floors, or walls except that a reasonable amount of small nails may be used to hang pictures in sheet rock or grooves in paneling; (iv) install new or additional telephone or television cables, outlets, or alarm systems; (v) install, alter, or change, any fixture; (vi) keep or permit any hazardous material on or near the Property, such as inflammable or explosive materials which might cause any fire or extended insurance coverage to be suspended or canceled or any premiums to be increased; (vii) dispose of any environmentally detrimental substance (for example, engine oil or radiator fluid) on the Property; or (viii) cause or allow any mechanic's or materialmen's lien to be filed against any portion of the Property or Lessee/Buyer's interest in this lease. Any additional items installed by Lessee/Buyer, including but not limited to additional smoke detectors, locks, fixtures, alarm systems, and cables, shall become the property of the Lessor/Seller.

(d) *Smoke Detectors: The Property contains at least one (1) smoke detector. Lessee/Buyer shall not remove or replace any smoke detector without Lessor/Seller's written permission. Lessee/Buyer shall regularly test the smoke detector(s). If Lessee/Buyer finds any smoke detector is not functioning, Lessee/Buyer shall immediately notify Lessor/Seller in writing. Lessor/Seller shall repair or replace the smoke detector(s) which are not functioning within a reasonable time after receipt of written notification from Lessee/Buyer. Lessee/Buyer shall replace all batteries in the smoke detector(s) at any time the batteries no longer function.*

(e) *Yard Maintenance:* Lessee/Buyer shall maintain, pay all expenses, and be responsible for all yard maintenance and use reasonable diligence in maintaining the yard, including but not limited to watering, mowing, fertilizing, edging, trimming, snow removal, and controlling all yard pests (fire ants, grub worms, fleas, and so forth). For the purposes of this lease, "yard" means all lawns, shrubbery, bushes, flowers, gardens, trees, rock or other landscaping, and other foliage on or encroaching on the Property or on any easement appurtenant to the Property.

(f) *Pool or Spa Maintenance:* Lessor/Seller shall maintain, pay all expenses, and be responsible for all pool and spa weekly/monthly maintenance and use reasonable diligence in maintaining the pool or spa, including but not limited to maintaining proper water heights, cleaning, sweeping, and all chemicals. Lessee/Buyer shall be responsible for repair or replacement of pool/spa equipment including but not limited to filters, pumps, cover, and sweeps and is restricted to the terms and conditions for repairs as stated in paragraph 16(b).

17. **LESSEE/BUYER'S REMEDIES FOR LESSOR/SELLER'S FAILURE TO REPAIR/ REMEDY A CONDITION:**
If Lessor/Seller has a legal duty to repair or remedy a condition materially affecting the physical health or safety of an ordinary tenant, Lessee/Buyer may terminate this lease, withhold rent, offset rent against needed repairs, or pursue judicial remedies *ONLY IF*: (a) Lessee/Buyer has given Lessor/Seller prior written notice to repair or remedy a condition which materially affects the physical health or safety of an ordinary tenant; (b) Lessor/Seller has had reasonable time to repair or remedy the condition (considering the nature of the problem and the reasonable availability of materials, labor, and utilities from a utility company); (c) Lessor/Seller has not made a diligent effort to repair or remedy the condition; (d) Lessee/Buyer has given subsequent written notice to Lessor/Seller stating the Lessee/Buyer intends to either terminate the lease if the condition is not repaired or remedied within seven (7) days after Lessor/Seller receives Lessee/Buyer's notice of intent to terminate, repair or remedy the condition and deduct the cost from the rent, or pursue judicial remedies; (e) Lessee/Buyer is not delinquent in the payment of rent when the notices are given; and (f) the condition would, in fact, materially affect the physical health or safety of an ordinary tenant.

18. **LIABILITY:** *Lessor/Seller shall NOT be responsible to Lessee/Buyer, Lessee/Buyer's guests, family, or occupants for any damages, injuries, or losses to person or property caused by fire, flood, water leaks, ice, snow, hail, winds, explosion, smoke, interruption of utilities, theft, burglary, robbery, assault, vandalism, other persons, condition of the Property, or other occurrences or casualty losses unless such damage or injury is caused by the gross negligence of Lessor/Seller. Lessee/Buyer agrees to hold Lessor/Seller harmless from any claims for damages no matter how caused, except for injury or damages for which Lessor/Seller is legally responsible, so long as Lessee/Buyer remains in possession of the Property. Lessee/Buyer shall promptly reimburse Lessor/Seller for any loss, property damage, or cost of repairs or service to the Property caused by negligence or by improper use by Lessee/Buyer, Lessee/Buyer's guests, family, or occupants unless Lessee/Buyer has made repairs pursuant to the procedures set forth in this lease. Lessor/Seller may require advance payment of repairs for with Lessee/Buyer is liable. NOTICE TO LESSEE/BUYER: Lessee/Buyer should secure Lessee/Buyer's own insurance coverage for protection against such liabilities and losses (_____ Lessee/Buyers initials).*

19. **ENCUMBRANCES:** *The only encumbrance(s) against the Property is(are):*

The parties agree that neither shall cause or permit any lien to attach to or exist on or against the Property which shall or may be superior to the rights of either party. Prior to the exercise of the option, Lessor/Seller reserves the right to change existing encumbrances on the Property through refinance, early payoff of the loan(s), or modifications of existing loans so long as the change would not create an encumbrance exceeding the agreed upon value of the Property.

20. **EXERCISE OF OPTION:** *The option may be exercised by Lessee/Buyer, if at all, as long as Lessee/Buyer is not in default of the terms and conditions of this agreement as enumerated under Paragraph 24. To exercise the option, Lessee/Buyer must notify Lessor/Seller in writing of such acceptance.*

21. **TITLE:**

    (a) *Within ten (10) working days upon receipt of written notification by Lessee/Buyer to exercise the option, Lessor/Seller shall execute and deliver to _____ all documents required to transfer title to the Property along with appropriate escrow instructions. Escrow shall be deemed "open" as of the date of Lessor/Seller's delivery.*

    (b) *Lessee/Buyer's duty to perform hereunder, after exercise of the option is contingent upon title to the Property being insurable as free and clear of all liens, encumbrances or other clouds on title to the Property, except:*

        (1) *General and special taxes for the fiscal year in which the escrow closes.*

        (2) *Exceptions, as agreed by Lessee/Buyer, to be contained in the title report and all current easements, covenants and restrictions of record.*

    (c) *Lessee/Buyer shall have five (5) days from receipt of a title report to examine the title to the Property and to report in writing any valid objections thereto. Any exceptions to the title which would be disclosed by examination of the record shall be deemed to have been accepted unless reported in writing within the five (5) days. If Lessee/Buyer objects to any exceptions to the title, Lessor/Seller shall use due diligence to remove such exceptions at their expense before close of escrow. But if such exceptions cannot be removed before close of escrow, all rights and obligations hereunder may, at the election of the Lessee/Buyer, terminate and end. Should Lessee/Buyer elect to rescind the agreement because of title exceptions, Lessor/Seller shall handle the initial option consideration of $ _____ as a deposit toward the Property and shall refund to the Lessee/Buyer the deposit minus an amount, if any, to repair damages to the Property caused by Lessee/Buyer. This refund shall occur only after Lessee/Buyer vacates the Property. At the expiration of the ten (10) day period for examination of title, Lessee/Buyer shall be deemed to have accepted such title in the absence of the required written objections.*

22. **ESCROW:**

    (a) *Upon both parties' agreement to consummate the sale, appropriate documents shall be recorded and escrow shall close within _____ days from the opening thereof. If escrow is not closed prior to the scheduled closing date or Lessee/Buyer has not complied with the terms of this agreement within _____ days after escrow is opened, escrow shall be canceled and this agreement shall be null and void. Lessee/Buyer, Lessor/Seller or escrow holder, as applicable, shall perform the following duties prior to close of escrow:*

(1) Lessor/Seller shall deliver to escrow holder an executed general warranty deed to the Property in recordable form conveying title in the Property to Lessee/Buyer.

(2) Escrow holder shall credit Lessee/Buyer with the OPTION CONSIDERATION accumulated and held by Lessor/Seller during the option period and the option consideration so credited shall be deducted from the required down payment.

(b) In the event Lessee/Buyer has exercised the option in the manner aforementioned herein, and Lessee/Buyer has not closed this escrow on the scheduled closing date for a reason other than Lessor/Seller's failure to deliver a general warranty deed to escrow holder as required by Paragraph 22 (a) (1) above, or the inability of escrow holder to obtain a policy of title insurance to insure title in Lessee/Buyer, subject only to those exceptions to title described in the policy of title or as otherwise described in Paragraph 21 above, then: (1) Lessee/Buyer shall have no right, title or interest in the Property; (2) Lessee/Buyer shall be liable to Lessor/Seller for all damages caused by Lessee/Buyer's wrongful failure to close escrow unless Lessor/Seller shall be in breach; (3) This escrow shall be automatically terminated without further instructions from any party; and (4) Escrow holder shall return all items to the party who deposited such items into escrow, without further instructions from either party hereto. Notwithstanding the above, Lessor/Seller may demand that Lessee/Buyer execute cancellation instructions prepared by escrow holder in the event an escrow established pursuant hereto is not closed on or before the scheduled closing date, for a reason other that described in this paragraph.

23. PRORATIONS, CLOSING COSTS, ASSUMPTION AND REFINANCING COSTS:

(a) Real property taxes on the Property and general and special assessments, if any, for the current fiscal year shall be prorated to the close of escrow.

(b) The "closing costs" shall be those costs incurred in conjunction with closing escrow and shall be paid at the close of escrow as follows:

(1) Lessor/Seller shall pay the following costs through escrow: real estate transfer tax, title exam and title guarantee premium, prorations due Lessee/Buyer, and one-half of the escrow fee (unless VA/FHA regulation prohibits payment of escrow fees by Lessee/Buyer in which case Lessor/Seller shall pay entire escrow fee).

(2) Lessee/Buyer shall secure new homeowner insurance. Lessee/Buyer shall pay one-half of the escrow fee, all of the assumption fees imposed by the secured lien holder(s), all loan discount points (if required), loan origination fees, appraisal fees, and all recording fees for the deed and any mortgage. If Lessee/Buyer wishes to obtain an owner's fee policy of title insurance, Lessee/Buyer shall pay the additional premium above the cost of the title guarantee.

(3) In the event escrow does not close on the scheduled closing date or another mutually agreed upon date thereafter, the closing costs incurred through the escrow to such date shall be the responsibility of the party at fault. In the event escrow shall fail to close on the scheduled closing date or another mutually agreed upon closing date due to fault of BOTH parties or NEITHER party to this agreement, the costs of terminating the escrow shall be divided equally between the parties.

24. DEFAULT BY LESSEE/BUYER AND ACCELERATION OF RENTS:

(a) The occurrence of any of the following shall constitute a material default and breach of lease by Lessee/Buyer.

(1) Monthly lease payments must be paid in a timely fashion, i.e. on or before the 1st day of each month. If Lessee/Buyer is more the THREE (3) days late on THREE (3) or more of the monthly payments and Lessor/Seller has not agreed in writing to extensions on the appropriate due dates, Lessor/Seller shall treat the failure to pay in a timely fashion as a breach of condition of the agreement and may refuse to convey title, even if there are no payments in default at the time Lessee/Buyer attempts to exercise the option to purchase. If the lease is in substantial default (50% or more of any monthly increment past due) at the time the option period matures, Lessor/Seller may refuse to convey title. CREDIT WORTHINESS OF LESSEE/BUYER IS OF THE ESSENCE IN THE LEASE-OPTION PORTION OF THIS CONTRACT. CREDIT WORTHINESS SHALL BE BASED UPON LESSEE/BUYER'S REGULAR AND TIMELY PAYMENTS OF MONTHLY LEASE OBLIGATIONS AS SPECIFIED ABOVE.

(2) Any failure by Lessee/Buyer to perform any other provision of this lease to be performed by Lessee/Buyer where such failure continues THIRTY (30) days after written notice thereof by Lessor/Seller shall constitute a material breach of this contract.

(b) If Lessee/Buyer fails to timely pay all rents due under this lease or otherwise fails to comply with this lease, Lessor/Seller may terminate this lease and/or Lessee/Buyer's right to occupy the Property by providing Lessee/Buyer with at least three (3) days written notice. Notice of termination may be by mail or personal delivery to Lessee/Buyer or left in a conspicuous place inside the Property. If Lessee/Buyer breaks this lease in any manner, or if Lessee/Buyer vacates the Property prior to the end of this lease or any renewal period, Lessee/Buyer shall be liable for all rents due under this lease and all rents which are payable during the remainder of this lease or renewal period shall be accelerated without notice or demand and shall be immediately due and payable and Lessee/Buyer shall, in addition to the accelerated rents, pay Lessor/Seller's cost of releasing the Property which the parties agree shall be $_____ as liquidated damages (not to exceed one month rent) for Lessor/Seller's time and inconvenience and fees necessary to release the Property. In the event of Lessee/Buyer's default, in addition to accelerated rents and cost of releasing, Lessee/Buyer shall pay all Lessor/Seller's costs associated with eviction of Lessee/Buyer, collection of unpaid or accelerated rent, late charges, returned check charges, repairs to the Property beyond normal wear and tear, attorneys' fees, court costs, prejudgment interest, and any other damages Lessor/Seller may be entitled by law. All amounts awarded by a court shall bear interest at the rate of 10% per annum. _Lessor/Seller may report unpaid rent or unpaid damages to credit report agencies._

25. **HOLDOVER:** *If Lessee/Buyer fails to vacate the Property on or before the termination date of this lease or at the end of any renewal period, Lessee/Buyer shall pay rent for the holdover period and shall indemnify Lessor/Seller and/or prospective tenants for damages, including lost rent, lodging expenses, and attorneys' fees. In the event of holdover, Lessor/Seller may extend this lease up to one month by notifying Lessee/Buyer, in writing. Rent for any holdover period shall be $_____ per day and shall be immediately due and payable on a daily basis and delinquent without notice or demand. Lessee/Buyer is in possession of the Property and liable for payment of rent for the holdover period until all keys, garage door openers, security codes, and other devices required to gain access to the Property are returned to Lessor/Seller and all of Lessee/Buyer's personal property is removed.*

26. **ASSIGNMENT AND SUBLETTING:** *Lessee/Buyer shall not assign or sublet the Property without Landlord's written consent. An assignment or subletting of the Property without Lessor/Seller's written consent shall be void and Lessor/Seller may terminate this lease. Under no circumstances shall Lessee/Buyer be released from Lessee/Buyer's obligations in this lease by virtue of an assignment or sublease.*

27. **SUBORDINATION:** *This lease and Lessee/Buyer's leasehold interest are and shall be subject, subordinate, and inferior to any lien or encumbrance now or hereafter placed on the Property by Lessor/Seller, to all advances made under any such lien or encumbrance, to the interest payable on any such lien or encumbrance, and to any and all renewals and extensions of any such lien or encumbrances.*

28. **CONTROLLING LAW:** *This lease shall be construed under and in accordance with laws of the State of _____ and all obligations of this lease are to be performed in the county in which the Property is located. In any lawsuit involving contractual or statutory obligations of Lessor/Seller or Lessee/Buyer, the prevailing party shall be entitled to recover attorneys' fees and all other costs of litigation from the non prevailing party. All amounts in any judgment shall bear 10% interest from the due date. Unless otherwise stated in this lease, all sums owed by Lessee/Buyer are due on demand.*

29. **REPRESENTATIONS:** *All Lessee/Buyer's statements in Lessee/Buyer's Application for Rental are material representations relied upon by Lessor/Seller. Any misrepresentation in this lease or in Lessee/Buyer's Application for Rental shall constitute a default of this lease and Lessor/Seller may terminate the lease and exercise Lessor/Seller's rights under paragraph 24.*

30. **ATTORNEY'S FEES:** *If Lessor/Seller or Lessee/Buyer is a prevailing party in any legal proceeding brought as a result of a dispute under this lease, such party shall be entitled to recover from the non-prevailing party all costs of such proceeding and reasonable attorneys' fees, unless otherwise specifically prohibited by statute.*

31. **JOINT AND SEVERAL LIABILITY:** *IF THERE IS MORE THAN ONE LESSEE/BUYER, EACH LESSEE/BUYER IS JOINTLY AND SEVERALLY LIABLE FOR EACH PROVISION OF THIS LEASE. Any act or notice to, or refund to, or the signature of, any one or more of the Lessee/Buyers, in relation to the renewal or termination of this lease, or with respect to any of the terms of this lease shall be fully binding on all the persons executing this lease as Lessee/Buyers. Each party signing this lease states that he or she is of legal age to enter into a binding contract for lodging.*

32. **TIME:** *Time is expressly declared to be of the essence in this lease.*

33. GENDER, TENSE AND PLURALITY OF WORDS: *All words used in the Agreement, including the words Lessor/Seller and Lessee/Buyer shall be construed to include the plural as well as the singular number; words used herein the present tense shall include the future as well as the present and words used in the masculine gender shall include the feminine and neuter.*

34. NOTICES: *Any and all notices and other communications required or permitted by this agreement shall be served on or given to either party by the other party in writing and shall be deemed duly served and given when personally delivered to any of the parties to whom it is directed, or in lieu of such personal service, when deposited in the United States mail first class postage prepaid, addressed to Lessor/Seller at _____ or Lessee/Buyer at the Property address or such forwarding address that Lessee/Buyer has given to Lessor/Seller.*

35. ENTIRE AGREEMENT, BINDING EFFECT, WAIVERS: *Lessor/Seller and Lessee/Buyer have not entered into any oral agreements and this written lease represents Lessor/Seller's and Lessee/Buyer's entire agreement. This lease shall not be modified unless by written agreement and signed by both parties. Any clause in this lease or addendum, if any, declared invalid by law shall not terminate or invalidate the remainder of this lease. This lease shall be binding upon and inure to the benefit of the parties to this lease and their respective heir, executors, administrators, legal representatives, successors, and permitted assigns. Lessor/Seller's past delay, waiver, or non enforcement of acceleration, contractual or statutory lien, rental due date, or any other right shall not be deemed to be a waiver of any other breach by Lessee/Buyer or any other term, condition, or covenant in this lease.*

36. SPECIAL PROVISIONS:

This is intended to be a legal agreement binding upon final acceptance. READ IT CAREFULLY. If you do not understand the effect of this lease, consult you attorney BEFORE signing.

_____   _____
LESSOR/SELLER   *DATE*   *LESSEE/BUYER*   *DATE*

_____   _____
LESSOR/SELLER   *DATE*   *LESSEE/BUYER*   *DATE*

Appendix III: Rental Expense Worksheet

	A	B	C	D	E	F	G	H	I	J	K	L	M	N	O	P
1						2003										
2																
3													Bank		Rcpt	
4	Date	Rent	Option	Maint.	Repairs	Suppls	Imp	Util	Advert	Interest	Taxes	Ins	Fees	Miles	No.	Description
5																
6		66508.36	4300.00	1139.04	3586.72	12091.69	0.00	3755.56	127.93	6945.73	8412.80	2443.60	1704.81	3554		
7																
8																
9	01-Jan	625.00	50.00													January rent
10	27-Jan				183.45										391	Furnace repair
11	01-Feb	425.00	50.00													February rent
12	01-Feb					18.06									392	Brass handles
13	01-Feb					211.86									393	Faucets for bathroom
14	05-Feb					8.50									394	Brass handles
15	05-Feb							64.14							395	Water bill (11/04/02 - 2/05/03)
16	05-Feb							124.76							396	Sewer bill (11/04/02 - 2/05/03)
17	07-Feb					35.18									397	Paint
18	07-Feb					18.84									398	Hinge for cabinet
19	01-Mar	813.90	50.00													399	March rent
20	15-Mar					6.82									400	Concrete patch
21	21-Mar					14.88									401	Concrete patch
22	22-Mar					32.15									402	Caulk and sealer
23	22-Mar					4.80									403	Vinyl patch
24	01-Apr	625.00	50.00													April rent
25	14-Apr					288.90									404	Topsoil and mulch
26	16-Apr					42.18									405	Fertilizer
27	19-Apr					4.01									406	Light bulbs
28	01-May	625.00	50.00													May rent
29	05-May							49.84							407	Water bill (2/05/03 - 5/05/03)
30	05-May							102.71							408	Sewer bill (2/05/03 - 5/05/03)
31	06-May					146.06									409	Carpet cleaning
32	01-Jun	625.00	50.00													June rent
33	06-Jun										586.40				410	Taxes for the 2nd half of 2002
34	26-Jun				1500.00										411	Electrical repairs for garage removal
35	26-Jun				4130.00										412	Demolish garage, remove driveway, etc.
36	01-Jul	777.55	50.00													July rent
37	19-Jul					88.96									413	Light bulbs, miscellaneous
38	29-Jul					106.00									414	Landscape services
39	01-Aug	625.00	50.00													August rent
40	22-Aug					140.91									416	Paint
41	22-Aug					73.71									417	Driveway sealer
42	07-Aug							46.37							418	Water bill (5/5/03 - 8/7/03)
43	07-Aug							96.67							419	Sewer bill (5/5/03 - 8/7/03)
44	19-Aug				114.95										420	Hot water tank repair
45	01-Sep	653.09	50.00													September rent + water/sewer - maint
46	01-Oct	625.00	50.00													October rent
47	29-Oct					45.59									421	Gutter/downspout supplies
48	31-Oct							46.37							422	Water bill (8/7/03 - 10/31/03)
49	31-Oct							96.67							423	Sewer bill (8/7/03 - 10/31/03)
50	01-Nov	625.00	50.00													November rent
51	04-Nov					2.85									424	Gutter elbow
52	04-Nov					36.48									425	Plumbing supplies
53	08-Nov					29.88									426	Electrical supplies
54	01-Dec	768.04	50.00													December rent + water/sewer
55	19-Dec					26.34									427	Timer and caulk
56	31-Dec												330.60			Insurance
57	31-Dec										621.42				428	Taxes for 1st half of 2003
58																
59																
60	Total	7812.58	600.00	0.00	5928.40	1382.96	0.00	627.53	0.00	0.00	1207.82	330.60	0.00	0		2003 Totals
61																
62		74320.94	4900.00	1139.04	9515.12	13474.65	0.00	4383.09	127.93	6945.73	9620.62	2774.20	1704.81	3554		
63																
64	Total 2003 Income			8412.58			Overall Total Income				79220.94					
65	Total 2003 Expenses			9477.31			Overall Total Expenses				49685.19					
66	Net Profit/Loss			-1064.73			Overall Net Profit/Loss				29535.75					
67																

About The Author

Tony and Sandy Midea ventured into the rental property business in 1993 with the purchase of their first single family home, and eventually expanded this business to include seven homes within two years. At present, they still possess one rental home. During the heyday of their rental property business, both were mid-level managers within large corporations, and managed the properties in their "spare time". Their experience with first hand management of these rental properties for the past 10 years forms the basis of knowledge for the book. The comical, light hearted writing style is derived from their playful senses of humor, and seeks to inform while entertaining.

The couple currently resides in Cleveland, OH.